From a Persian Kitchen

From a Persian Kitchen

FRESH DISCOVERIES IN IRANIAN COOKING

Jila Dana-Haeri

I.B. TAURIS
LONDON · NEW YORK

Published in 2014 by I.B.Tauris & Co. Ltd
6 Salem Road, London W2 4BU
175 Fifth Avenue, New York NY 10010
www.ibtauris.com

Distributed in the United States and Canada
exclusively by Palgrave Macmillan
175 Fifth Avenue, New York NY 10010

ISBN   978 1 78076 801 4

A full CIP record for this book is available from the British Library
A full CIP record is available from the Library of Congress
Library of Congress Catalog Card Number: available

Typeset in Monotype Fournier by illuminati, Grosmont
Printed and bound in Italy by Printer Trento S.r.l.

Contents

Acknowledgements

THIS BOOK would not have been possible without the tremendous encouragement and support of John Bateson. Throughout the process of this book's creation he meticulously edited the recipes and gave invaluable advice. He also contributed his wonderful Persian ice cream recipe, acclaimed among our friends.

My special thanks to Simon Bunegar for his wonderful photography, which has brought these recipes to life.

For my country, whose food I relish
as I remember her green hills and dusty open deserts,
her snowy mountains and warm seas

Preface

FOOD and the rituals around its preparation, cooking
and eating form a substantial part of social relations
and common identity. They punctuate daily life and also
special occasions, from festivities to death. The memory
of events is often food-related, as though food helps us put
together bits of the past and give it cohesion.

In Iran the 'know-how' of cooking went from generation
to generation in warm, crowded kitchens where it passed
from grandmothers and family cooks to children and
grandchildren, who all participated in cooking the family
meals. This meant that there was not the tradition of well-
documented cookbooks that we see in the West. However,
since the Islamic Revolution and on account of the growing
diaspora a number of cookbooks have been published
documenting recipes which previously were only known in
family circles.

In my previous book, *New Persian Cooking*, I introduced
recipes which are, in general, my variations on well-known
Persian dishes that are cooked all over the country. My aim
was to make Persian cooking easy by adapting it to new,
less time-consuming methods and replacing difficult-to-find
ingredients with those readily available in the West.

Being one of the oldest and greatest empires, Persia has
a diverse culture comprising different tribes, traditions and
customs. This is reflected in the cuisine, in terms of both
ingredients used and methods of cooking. In this book my
aim is to highlight the variety and diversity of recipes, from

the dishes originating in the north to those of the south. The north, by the Caspian Sea, with high rainfall and temperate climate, is covered with orchards. The dishes are predominantly rich in herbs and are often sweet-and-sour in taste.

As we go from north to south rainfall dwindles, the weather is hot and dry. The culinary tradition is influenced by aromatic and hot spices.

How to use this book

This is not, however, a regional cookbook. Rather, I hope to demonstrate the diversity of the cuisine by juxtaposing sweet-and-sour with spicy and aromatic dishes.

CHAPTER 1 starts by introducing the diversity of the Persian table, the particularities of Persian cooking, including *aash* (traditional thick soup), *khoresh* (the Persian equivalent to stews and casseroles) and *polo* (Persian rice). The centrality of herbs in Persian cooking is explained.

CHAPTER 2 includes recipes for *aashes*, *aabgusht* (lamb soup) and *eshkeneh* (egg soup). *Aash* is a rich soup with a thick consistency. Although *aashes* are made all over the country, the recipes vary depending on the region and the seasonal availability of herbs. *Aashes* are nutritious meals that can be served as a main course with bread. *Aabgusht*, lamb soup with pulses, is an old dish which was traditionally served in caravanserai (old inns with a central courtyard, used by caravans stopping for the night) and tea houses. *Eshkeneh* is a thin egg soup, traditionally made with onions and fenugreek. It can, however, be made with different herbs and fruits. *Eshkenehs* are more popular in the north; the addition of egg to the soup is probably due to Chinese influence.

CHAPTER 3 introduces the *khoreshes*. *Khoresh* is a rich sauce, almost always served with plain rice. The nearest equivalent in the West would be stew or casserole. *Khoresh* can be made with meat, chicken or fish, combined with

vegetables, herbs, fruits or pulses. The chapter is divided
into sweet-and-sour and aromatic and spicy *khoresh* recipes.
For a typical example of a sweet-and-sour *khoresh*, see
naaz khatoon, which is lamb with herbs and aubergine in a
sweet-and-sour sauce, a northern speciality. An example of
a southern speciality *khoresh* from Bushehr, by the Persian
Gulf, is *khoresh-e morgh va seebzamini ba curry*.

CHAPTER 4 consists of recipes for *khorak*, which in Farsi
means food and refers to a variety of dishes made of meat,
chicken, fish or vegetables. The method of cooking also
varies, from roasting to grilling, frying and stewing. *Khoraks*
always have very little or no sauce at all. They are usually
eaten with bread. This chapter, too, is divided into sweet-
and-sour and spicy *khoraks*.

CHAPTER 5 is devoted to rice. Rice is the hallmark of
Persian cuisine. Great attention is paid to the preparation and
presentation of rice dishes. A dish of rice should be aesthetically pleasing as well as exciting the appetite by its aroma.
This chapter describes the unique texture and diversity
of Persian rice and the different methods of preparing
and cooking it, including the delicious *tahdig* (crust at the
bottom). The recipes in this chapter are also divided into
sweet-and-sour dishes, for example *haveej polo* (saffron carrot
rice), and savoury aromatic rice such as *beriani Bushehri*.
Rice dishes provide tasty accompaniments to meat, poultry
or fish dishes, as well as main vegetarian courses; some are
standalone main rice courses.

CHAPTER 6 provides recipes for appetisers and accompaniments and introduces Persian food customs and
rituals. The importance of appetisers, nibbles and other
accompaniments like pickles is emphasised as they constitute
an essential part of the meal; they help to cleanse the palate
between each dish and also create a balanced diet. A fresh
bouquet of herbs is almost always brought to the table
accompanied by a block of shimmering white feta cheese and

one or two yogurt dishes. These provide the vitamins and antioxidants to boost the immune system on a daily basis. The benefits of natural set yogurt, as probiotic, have only recently been brought to the attention of the West, whereas it has always been valued by Persians for its medicinal qualities.

CHAPTER 7 deals with side dishes, salads and yogurt-based dishes called *borani*. *Borani* consists of a cooked and fried vegetable, with plenty of garlic, mixed in yogurt. There are different varieties of *borani* depending on the vegetables used. *Boranis* are popular all over the country, although the proportion of vegetables and garlic differ according to region. Some of the salads can be served as a starter or light lunch. The side dishes of yogurt, salad and fresh herbs contribute to maintaining a balanced and healthy diet.

CHAPTER 8 features *shirini*, which means literally 'sweet things': puddings, ice creams and jams. Although Persians do not have the tradition of eating a dessert course, they are lovers of *shirini* (sweet nibbles) served with tea after the meal. Ice creams and sorbets are traditionally eaten as snacks in the afternoon or on summer evenings.

Recently, with increasing Western influence, sweet dishes and ice creams are served as Western-style desserts. This chapter includes a variety of ice creams, puddings and sweet nibbles. Jams and preserves are made from a range of fruits and vegetables, such as carrot and cucumber; they are served alone or as a topping for ice cream, and are rarely eaten with bread!

The ceremonial table
of Norooz, the Persian
New Year

CHAPTER I

The diversity of the Persian table

PERSIAN CULTURE has always been a source of mystery, intrigue and discovery – whether it is a walk at sunrise in the serene but dust-ridden ruins of Persepolis, an evening's casual reading of poetry leaning on a divan covered with hand-woven carpets, placed between rose beds in a scented garden in Shiraz, or a structured tour around Isfahan's unique architectural masterpieces that have attracted visitors for centuries. The murmur of Hafez poetry, Mawlana's (Rumi) story of eternal love and Khayyam's message of seizing the moment touch the heart of even the most unfamiliar traveller. Walking amid the hustle and bustle of Iran's many labyrinthine bazaars, one experiences complex melanges of aroma from saffron to cardamom, rose water to *beedeh meshk* to orange blossom, and vibrant colours from *zardchobeh* (turmeric) to *sumac* and *zereshk* (barberry) to pomegranate.

While many people are familiar with the history, literature, philosophy and spiritual characteristics of Persia, the cuisine has not been well known in the West until recently. For the curious observer who knows Iran as one of the oldest wine-producing countries, it is intriguing to know how culinary activities have developed, what are the types and peculiarities of cooking, and how this rich and complex culture is reflected in its food.

PREVIOUS SPREAD
Apple blossom in one of the orchards scattered across the north of Iran

The impact of geography and history

The birthplace of Persian cookery has covered, at various times in its existence, an area beyond the Caspian Sea to the north, the Persian Gulf and some coastal regions to the south, India and China to the east, extending to the west to include parts of Egypt and Europe. Under different dynasties over the past three millennia, Persia was one of the oldest and greatest empires. Persia has also been subjected to repeated invasion from near and from afar, which has led to the creation of a diverse culture comprising different tribes, traditions and behaviours. This has been reflected to a large extent in the diversity of the cuisine, in terms of both ingredients and methods of cooking.

The country we now call Iran is a vast plateau with an area of 636,000 square miles. In the north it borders the Caspian Sea and in the south the Gulf of Oman and the Persian Gulf, a distance of more than 1,000 miles. It is encircled by high mountain ranges, which to a great degree determine where the rain falls.

The climate of this vast area is varied. In the north-west (bordering Azerbaijan and Turkey) and north-east (bordering Afghanistan and Turkmenistan) winters are cold with heavy snowfall and freezing temperatures. The northern provinces bordering the Caspian Sea enjoy a temperate climate with high rainfall. In the northern half of the country spring and autumn are relatively mild, while summers are dry and hot. In the south the climate is very different: winters are mild with little rainfall; summers are very dry and hot.

The country's geography, its varied climate and topographical particularities, from lush and mountainous terrain to flat and arid desert, have produced a wide range of agricultural produce, from rice (grown in the northern provinces by the Caspian Sea with their high rainfall) to

wheat and sugar cane (in the western provinces), to apples,
cherries, peaches (the Khorasan region in the north-east),
pomegranates (central western provinces), citrus fruits (north
and south); the central province of Isfahan is famous for a
special type of melon and for its peaches.

The combination of diverse historical traditions and geo-
graphical conditions has led to the creation and subsequent
evolution of a cuisine with distinct regional variations in
terms of variety of tastes and subtlety of flavours. No matter
where you are in Iran, the combination of herbs and spices
with main ingredients creates multiple layers of taste and
aroma, delicately balanced so that none is dominant over the
others and allowing flavours and textures to complement one
another. Tastes and flavours vary, however, with each region
adding its signature to the recipe.

The north, with its high rainfall and temperate climate,
is lush with herbs and orchards. Historically straddling the
route of the Silk Road, northern cuisine has been influenced
by the other countries it passes through, such as China. The
resultant dishes are predominantly rich in herbs and are often
sweet-and-sour in taste. Dried and fresh fruits and nuts are
an essential part of cooking here; herbs like mint, tarragon
and parsley play a dominant role.

Moving south, rainfall decreases, giving way to hot, dry
weather. The culinary tradition further south is influenced
by aromatic and hot spices, due to the important spice trade
with India. The resultant sauces are rich in tamarind juice,
curry spices and the dominant herbs coriander (cilantro) and
fenugreek.

The recipes in my previous book, *New Persian Cooking*,
are well known across the whole of Iran. They are a common
language. Everyone knows 'national dishes' such as *ghormeh
sabzi* or *ghiemeh*. These might be interpreted differently in
different regions but every Iranian would recognise them.
Consequently they are cooked by most members of the

Iranian diaspora and are also among the most common recipes cooked by Western enthusiasts of Persian food.

The aim of the present book, however, is to highlight the variety and diversity of recipes, from sweet-and-sour in the north to spicy and aromatic in the south. But my primary concern is not where each particular dish comes from. A good recipe moves around very quickly; it is passed from one person to another, across the country, regardless of its regional origin.

It should also be remembered that each family has its own unique way of cooking a dish, which could therefore be very different from the same dish cooked in another family. This is because in Iran cooking knowledge was traditionally transferred verbally among members of the family, particularly from mother to daughter. The outcome in all cases, though, is to combine ingredients in a way that creates fine layers of texture, taste and aroma.

Coming from a family that has roots in both the south and the north I have been lucky enough to be able to choose recipes that I first tasted either in my paternal grandfather's house in the north or in my southern maternal home. I have replaced some of the ingredients with ones more readily available in the West and have made them as compatible as possible with the time constraints of modern cooking and with modern cooking equipment.

Distinctive features of Persian cuisine

Despite the enormous diversity of dishes and methods of cooking, the basic features of Persian cuisine are the same all over the country. All regions, from north to south, east and west, cook *aash*, *khoresh*, *khorak* and rice, the key dishes that are particular to the Persian culinary tradition. These are usually served with yogurt dishes and other accompaniments and the meal is finished with *shirini*, literally 'sweet things'.

Aash

Aashes are rich, nutritious soups with a thick consistency similar to porridge. The importance of *aash* in Persian cuisine is such that in Farsi a cook is called *aashpaz*, meaning 'the one who knows how to make *aash*'!

Aashes are cooked all over the country, each region having its own favourite. For example, in the north the *aashes* are rich with herbs and fruits and the dominant taste is sweet-and-sour; in the south they tend to use fewer herbs and the *aashes* are more sour than sweet. The difference between *aashes* in the two regions is best illustrated by *pahti*, beetroot and pulse soup, which in the south is hot and spicy with the addition of tamarind juice and coriander, whilst in the north they make it with pomegranate syrup, without coriander and chilli (see p. 27 for the southern version).

Khoresh

Khoresh or *khoresht* is a rich sauce, almost always served with plain rice. The nearest equivalent in the West is stew or casserole, although these would probably contain more meat than a traditional *khoresh*. *Khoresh* can be made with meat or fish and be combined with vegetables, herbs, fruits or pulses.

Since meat is the most expensive ingredient in a meal, the quantity required would be less when mixed with pulses, herbs or vegetables. A further benefit of such a combination is a healthier diet, with the addition of vitamins, minerals and other proteins to the meat dish.

The diversity of sweet-and-sour, aromatic and spicy, also applies to *khoreshes*. A typical example of a sweet-and-sour *khoresh* is *naaz khatoon*, lamb with herbs and aubergine in a sweet-and-sour sauce, which originated in the north (p. 57). An example of a dish that originated in the south is a *khoresh* from Bushehr, featuring spicy coriander: *aaloo gashneez* (p. 77). The dominant herbs in *naaz khatoon* are parsley and mint, in contrast to the coriander of the southern-origin *khoresh*.

Historically, in the provinces by the Caspian Sea in the north, *khoreshes* with fruits like quince, apple and prune and vegetables like rhubarb were very popular. In the south, potato and tomato and vegetables like okra were the dominant ingredients. Again, the seasoning in the north was predominantly citrus juice or pomegranate syrup. In the south, tamarind juice was the preferred choice.

Rice

Rice is the hallmark of Persian cuisine. Great attention is paid to the preparation and presentation of rice dishes. It is important for the rice grains to be fully elongated (*qad keshideh*) and separate. A dish of rice should be aesthetically pleasing as well as exciting the appetite with its aroma. Just as it is important for the rice grains to be perfectly cooked through without any stickiness, it is also important for the other ingredients mixed in with the rice to be cooked but remain whole and recognisable. The beauty of *morassa polo* (jewelled rice, p. 143), for example, is in the juxtaposition of the bright ruby-coloured barberry with the green pistachio, orange and carrot juliennes scattered in the saffron rice. Even plain rice is decorated with saffron to lend it more visual interest.

There are also sticky rice dishes called *dami* or *dampokht*, which are usually cooked for informal occasions. These started life in the north, as rice is grown in the provinces by the Caspian Sea and has long been the staple food of these regions. However, a spicy and aromatic version of *lakh lakh* (sticky rice with fish, p. 162) is a 'poor man's dish' which was taught to me in my southern home.

The diversity of rice dishes is illustrated by *kalam polo* (cabbage rice, p. 141). The version I learnt in my northern

Roast poussin with cherry tomatoes and tomato rice, a summery lunch combination

home, for example, contains sultanas, which gives it a tinge of sweetness; however, the dish I learnt to make in the south (*kalam polo Shirazi*; see the recipe in *New Persian Cooking*) contains dill and other aromatic herbs and is not sweet.

The centrality of herbs in Persian cuisine

Herbs play an integral role in Persian cooking. The amounts used often seem incredible to non-Iranians. Herbs serve as the building blocks of most dishes and are used in abundance: they are added to rice, constitute the main ingredient of *khoreshes*, and are the principal component of the stuffing mixes for *khoraks*. They are also eaten raw as an accompaniment to most meals.

In the Persian kitchen one encounters a mountain of herbs. As Margaret Shaida describes in *The Legendary Cuisine of Persia*, herbs are sold in kilograms rather than as a few sprigs. As she so beautifully puts it, 'The way Persians utilise herbs is not for the faint hearted!' This is especially true when the time comes to chop them, often finely, as is the requirement for most herb dishes.

In Iran, herbs are bought daily, having been freshly picked and brought to the shaded markets and kept cool by sprinkling water. I still remember the herb market in Bushehr, on the Persian Gulf, where stand after stand sold coriander, parsley, mint, basil, chives, tarragon, and many more, each made into large bundles and arranged in hessian baskets. The market felt fresh with the scent of mint mixed with basil, and cool in the heat of a summer morning.

The Persian *sofreh*

Until the middle of the last century, in most houses the tradition was to sit on the floor to eat. Floors were covered with thick Persian carpets and there were large cushions scattered around to sit and to lean on. Meals were eaten on

Paneer, gherdo va sabzi, herb plate with feta and walnut, is an ever-present dish on Persian tables

the *sofreh* – a tablecloth, spread on the carpet over a thick cover, possibly of leather.

Although styles of cooking are vastly diverse, reflecting particularities of each region, there is a common theme in the way food is served and eaten all over the country: everything is brought to the table or the *sofreh* at the same time – *aash*, rice and *khoresh*, fresh herbs, yogurt, salads, bread and feta cheese. People serve themselves as they like; no strict order is followed. One might take what in the West is considered the main course, like rice and *khoresh*, before *aash*, which in the West would be considered a starter, or go back to the latter having partaken of the 'main course'.

In Persian households, more than one dish is cooked even for everyday meals. For example, a *khoresh* will usually have rice with it; furthermore, there will always be present, even for the simplest of meals, a side dish of yogurt, either plain or mixed with vegetables (*borani*, p. 207), a bowl of fresh herbs, and pickles of some sort.

For dinner parties and festivities an array of appetising nibbles and accompaniments are set on the table. There would be at least two rice dishes and two different *khoreshes* or *khoraks*. It is unheard of – indeed would be considered overly frugal – to serve only one dish.

Accompaniments and side dishes are an essential part of the meal; they serve to cleanse the palate between each dish and help create a balanced diet. A fresh bouquet of herbs, typically consisting of mint, tarragon, basil, watercress, spring onions and radishes, would almost always be brought to the table, together with a block of feta cheese. A small parcel made of cheese and fresh herbs wrapped in a piece of bread can be an appetiser or enjoyed at the end of the meal.

Although, strictly speaking, Persian cuisine does not put much emphasis on desserts, Persians are lovers of *shirini* (sweet nibbles). Perfectly brewed tea and sweet nibbles are usually served after the *sofreh* has been cleared. Tea is served in *estekaan* – small slim-waisted glass tumblers – to show its ruby colour. The sweets, almost always homemade, include almond marzipan (*toot*, p. 230) *baklava* and *suhan* (p. 237). Jams are also eaten as dessert, on their own or with yogurt. Ice creams are now a popular addition to the *shirini*, often served with a spoonful of jam.

The importance of wine

The ancient Persians were great lovers of wine. King Darius's throne is said to have been placed in the shadow of a golden vine with precious stones representing the fruit.

The tradition of wine-making in Iran dates back thousands of years. An inscription in Persepolis (the capital of the Achaemenid Empire in 500 BCE) indicates that sweet and ordinary wines were delivered daily to the royal household. The traditional Persian grape Shiraz (Syrah) is nowadays grown all over the world. It makes a rich red wine that goes well with most Persian dishes.

Persian literature is all the richer for references to wine, whether it be the nectar of enlightenment or a refuge from the ills of the world. As our most famous poet Hafez, of the fourteenth century, says:

> Saaghi! Set our grail ablaze with your lustrous wine
> Minstrel! Ring the note of this rising fortune of mine
> For the beloved's image in the cup we have found
> Oh ignorant of blissful ecstasy without bound
> Eternal is he, whom in love rejoices his heart
> Our perpetuity in the book of life we chart
> Drunkenness is sweet in our beloved's hazy eyes
> For this to wine we gladly yield the rein of our lives.

I hope this book has achieved my aim of introducing less famous but equally delicious recipes to a wider audience. I also hope that the book has, to some extent, shown the diversity of Persian cuisine. These dishes have been a trip down memory lane for me. I hope that you also enjoy cooking from these recipes and making them your own.

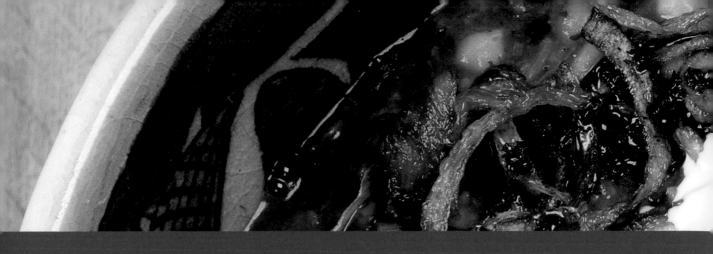

CHAPTER 2

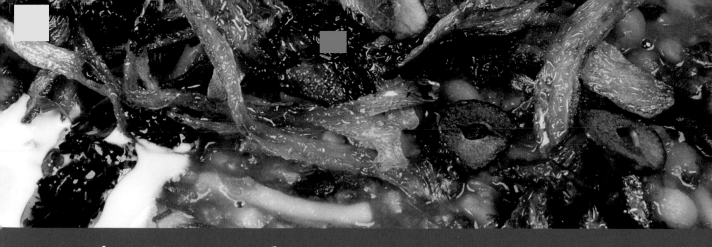

Aashes, aabgushts and eshkenehs

AASHES

AASHES are a feature of Persian cuisine that is cooked all over the country, although each region has its own favourite. They are thick soups with a consistency similar to that of porridge. The secret of a good *aash* is to get the base mixture right; this consists of split peas, pulses, rice, onions and a variety of fresh herbs. The onions should be fried until golden brown to lend their aroma and taste to the final product. The rice and pulses are cooked until completely soft, creating a creamy texture.

There are many combinations and permutations of the ingredients, depending on the region and the seasonal availability of herbs.

Although almost all *aashes* can be cooked as vegetarian dishes using vegetable stock, the use of chicken stock will give them a richer taste. *Aash* is very nutritious due to its mix of pulses and herbs, a good source of protein and carbohydrate. It can be eaten as a main meal with bread.

Dill and yogurt soup

Aash-e maast

SERVES 6–8
PREPARATION about 20
    minutes
COOKING about 2 hours

INGREDIENTS

200 g/7 oz split peas
150 g/5 oz rice
120 g/4 oz dill (or 4
  tablespoons dried dill)
1 medium-sized onion
2½ litres/4 pints chicken or
    vegetable stock
1 teaspoon turmeric
450 g/1 lb Greek-style yogurt
5 tablespoons lemon juice
30 g/1 oz butter
4 tablespoons vegetable oil
salt and pepper

GARNISH

1 large onion
1 tablespoon dried mint
3 cloves of garlic, finely
    chopped
4 tablespoons vegetable oil

This is a very smooth, aromatic and creamy soup. My friends refer to it as 'Jila's *aash*'. It has become the staple of our parties and festivities.

My recipe is different from the traditional one inasmuch as dill is the main herb used, rather than the customary mix of parsley, coriander, chives and spinach. This is an easy *aash* to prepare and can be made all year round, replacing fresh dill with the dried version if necessary.

PREPARATION

Wash the split peas in cold water, add boiling water and let them soak for at least a couple of hours. Wash the rice repeatedly in cold, salted water and soak.

If using fresh dill, wash it and dry in a salad crisper. Pinch off the leaves and tender stalks and discard the thicker, tougher ones. Pile the leaves on a chopping board and chop them finely with a sharp wide-bladed knife.

Peel and finely chop the onion.

COOKING

In a large heavy-based saucepan melt the butter; add the oil and heat up. Fry the chopped onion until soft and golden. Drain the split peas and add to the pan with the turmeric. Stir a couple of times and then pour in about half of the chicken or vegetable (for the vegetarian option) stock. Bring to the boil. Put the lid on and reduce the heat. Allow to simmer until the split peas are completely cooked (approximately 1 hour). *No salt should be added at this stage.* Once the split peas are cooked, drain the rice and add to the

saucepan. Add the rest of the stock and allow to simmer for a further half an hour. Stir occasionally to stop the mixture from sticking to the bottom of the pan. When the rice is almost so soft that you cannot distinguish the grains, add the finely chopped fresh (or dried) dill. The mixture should be creamy and thick at this stage. Add small amounts of boiling water to adjust the consistency if needed (more water will make the soup thinner). Allow to simmer for 30 minutes on a low heat, stirring occasionally. Then remove from the heat and allow to stand for five minutes. Mix the lemon juice with the yogurt and add to the pan, stirring all the while to mix thoroughly. Taste and adjust the seasoning as necessary. Keep warm; the *aash* is served hot.

GARNISH

Fry the onion in 2 tablespoons of oil until light brown. Add the chopped garlic, stir and put to one side. In another small frying pan, heat up the rest of the oil. Add the dried mint. Stir and remove from the heat immediately. Serve the *aash* in a soup bowl and decorate with both garnishes.

Beetroot, mung bean and black-eyed bean *aash*

Pahti

Pahti is a very nutritious hearty soup from Bushehr. Originally it was a peasant dish, as it contains a few cheap, readily available ingredients. It is cooked using tamarind juice, which is typically used in the south. Tamarind is believed to have come to Iran through trade with India. In the northern version of *pahti* the tamarind is replaced with pomegranate syrup and no chilli is used.

This is a perfect vegetarian meal.

PREPARATION

Soak the mung beans and the black-eyed beans in cold water overnight.

If using uncooked beetroots, wash and peel them. Chop the beetroot into 1 cm/½ inch cubes and set to one side. Peel and chop the onions and the garlic. Chop the chilli.

Dissolve the tamarind paste in 500 ml/1 pint boiling water.

Wash the beetroot or spinach leaves and remove the tough stalks. With a wide-bladed knife finely chop the leaves. Wash the coriander and dry it in a salad crisper. Pinch off the leaves and tender stalks and discard the thicker, tougher ones. Pile the leaves on a chopping board and finely chop them with a sharp wide-bladed knife.

COOKING

In a large heavy-based pan that can accommodate all the ingredients as they expand, heat 2 tablespoons of vegetable oil and fry half of the chopped onion until translucent. Drain the mung and black-eyed beans and add to the pan, stir,

SERVES 6–8
PREPARATION about 30 minutes plus soaking
COOKING about 2½ hours

INGREDIENTS

150 g/5 oz mung beans
150 g/5 oz black-eyed beans
300 g/11 oz beetroot (raw or cooked)
500 g/1 lb 2 oz beetroot leaves or spinach
150 g/5 oz coriander/cilantro
5 cloves of garlic
2 medium onions
1–2 hot chillies
1 teaspoon turmeric
70 g/2½ oz tamarind paste
500 ml/1 pint vegetable stock
2 litres/3½ pints boiling water
4 tablespoons vegetable oil
30 g/1 oz butter

GARNISH (OPTIONAL)

2 tablespoons vegetable oil
4 cloves of garlic, chopped

pour in 1½ litres/2½ pints of boiling water and bring back
to the boil. Reduce the heat and simmer for approximately
1 hour. If using raw beetroot add it to the pan at this stage.
Simmer for another 30–40 minutes until all the ingredients
are cooked.

Meanwhile, in a frying pan heat 2 tablespoons of the oil
and fry the rest of the onions until golden (approximately 5
minutes), then add the garlic, the chilli and the turmeric and
stir fry for a couple of minutes. Add the chopped coriander,
stir well, fry for a couple of minutes and set side.

Add the chopped beetroot or spinach leaves, coriander
mix, vegetable stock and tamarind juice to the pan with the
beans. If using cooked beetroots add them to the pan at this
stage. Season well with salt and pepper and allow to simmer
gently for 40–45 minutes. Add more water if the soup has
gone too thick at this stage – it should have a thick hearty
consistency but should still be liquid. Remove from the heat,
check the seasoning and allow to stand for 10–15 minutes
before serving.

GARNISH

Heat the oil and stir-fry the chopped garlic.

Pahti has the dark red colour of beetroot, mixed with the
green of the leaves and dark tamarind juice. Serve in a large
bowl; pour the fried garlic over. *Pahti* is delicious with warm
flatbread, a hot pickle and a side dish of plain yogurt.

Noodle soup

Aash-e reshteh

SERVES 6–8
PREPARATION about 30–35 minutes plus soaking
COOKING about 2½ hours

INGREDIENTS

1 large onion
50 g/2 oz mung beans
50 g/2 oz split peas
50 g/2 oz green lentils
50 g/2 oz red kidney beans
    (or a 450 g/1 lb can)
50 g/2 oz chick peas
    (or a 450 g/1 lb can)
50 g/2 oz rice
150 g/5 oz spinach or beetroot
    leaves
100 g/3½ oz dill
100 g/3½ oz coriander/cilantro
100 g/3½ oz parsley
100 g/3½ oz chives
    (or the green ends of
    spring onions)
50 g/2 oz tarragon
    (2 tablespoons if using
    dried) or 30 g/1 oz *marzeh*
    (summer savoury)
100 g/3½ oz Persian wheat
    noodles
1 teaspoon turmeric
4 tablespoons vegetable oil
50 g/2 oz butter
2 litres/3½ pints boiling water
3 chicken or vegetable stock
    cubes
salt and pepper

This a very old *aash*, going right back to Achaemenid Persia (550 BCE). It is believed that Zoroastrians made this *aash* to celebrate the first day of the month. The noodle symbolises the path that leads to an auspicious result; when they faced a difficulty, Zoroastrians made this soup in the hope of finding the right answer.

In Islamic Iran *aash-e reshteh* is cooked in religious festivities and to give thanksgiving to God when a pledge (a *nazre*) is fulfilled.

This soup is very hearty, rich with pulses and herbs, and of course the addition of noodles makes it even richer. Wheat flour noodles are used for this *aash*; these can be obtained from Persian food shops.

Canned red kidney beans and canned chick peas can be used instead of dried ones; add them to the *aash* at the last stage of cooking.

PREPARATION

This is the time-consuming part of the recipe. Measure all the pulses; wash them a few times and soak them all in cold water overnight.

Measure the rice and wash it thoroughly and repeatedly until the water is reasonably clear. Leave it to soak for a couple of hours in salted water.

To prepare the herbs, wash them in plenty of cold water and dry them thoroughly to make them easier to chop. Put the herbs on a tray and pinch the leaves and tender stalks to separate them from the tougher stalks. Discard wilting and yellowing leaves. Using a sharp wide-bladed knife, finely chop the herbs. The mountain of leaves you started off with should be reduced to a hillock when you finish. Set to one side. If you have chopped the herbs a few hours before cooking you can keep them fresh by covering them with a wet tea towel and putting them in the fridge.

GARNISH

4 tablespoons vegetable oil
1 medium onion
1 tablespoon dried mint
1 tablespoon *kashk* (see INGREDIENTS) or Greek-style yogurt

COOKING

Choose a heavy-based saucepan that is big and deep enough to accommodate all the ingredients. It needs to be big because the pulses expand considerably when cooked; the heavy base ensures an even distribution of heat. Put the pan on a medium to high heat and melt the butter. Add the oil and fry the onion in the butter and oil mixture until soft and golden. Drain the pulses and add them to the onions. Stir a couple of times to cover them in oil. Add about a litre/2 pints of the boiling water and bring back to the boil. Cover the pan with a lid and reduce the heat. To help the pulses to cook faster no salt should be added at this stage.

Allow to simmer for approximately an hour and a half until all the pulses are cooked. Drain the rice and add to the pan with the stock cubes (use vegetable stock cubes for a vegetarian option) and the rest of the water. Simmer for 30 minutes until the rice is cooked, stirring occasionally to stop the mixture from sticking to the bottom of the pan. When the rice is completely softened (and you cannot distinguish the grains), add the herbs and the turmeric.

Allow to simmer gently on a low heat for another 30 minutes while stirring frequently. It is important to cook this *aash* slowly for the aroma of the herbs to develop and be diffused into the dish. If using canned pulses, add them after this time. At this stage fold in the noodles, adding more boiling water if the consistency is too thick, and simmer for 10 more minutes, stirring frequently.

GARNISH

Fry the onion in 3 tablespoons of oil until light brown; set to one side. In another small frying pan, heat up the butter and the rest of the oil. Add the dry mint. Stir and remove from the heat immediately. Serve the *aash* in a soup bowl and decorate with mint and onion garnishes. If using *kashk* or yogurt, you can either put 4–5 blobs on the top of the bowl or, alternatively, offer a bowl of *kashk* or yogurt separately to be used as required.

Aash-e reshteh

Thick mung bean soup

Aash-e maash

Mung beans are the basic ingredient of many *aashes*. This *aash* with added turnips and spinach is a hearty soup for cold winter days.

PREPARATION

Measure the rice and wash it repeatedly until the water is reasonably clear. Leave it to soak for 30 minutes in salted water.

Wash the mung beans and set to one side.

To prepare the herbs, wash them in plenty of cold water then dry. Put the herbs on a tray and pinch off the leaves and tender stalks to separate them from the tougher stalks. Discard wilting and yellowing leaves. Using a sharp wide-bladed knife, finely chop the herbs.

Peel and slice the onion and cut the turnips into 4 pieces.

COOKING

Choose a large saucepan, which is deep enough to allow room for expansion of the ingredients. A heavy-based saucepan is ideal. Melt the butter, add the oil and heat up. Fry the chopped onion until soft and golden. Add the turmeric and stir well. Add the drained rice and the mung beans; stir to mix all the ingredients and pour in the stock. Bring to the boil, reduce the heat, cover and simmer for 30–40 minutes. The mung beans should be soft at this stage and the soup should have the consistency of porridge. Add the turnip pieces and the chopped herbs, mix well and simmer for a further 30 minutes until the turnips are tender. Add the lemon juice.

SERVES 6–8
PREPARATION about 30 minutes plus soaking
COOKING about 1¼ hours

INGREDIENTS

100 g/3½ oz mung beans
50 g/2 oz rice
1 medium onion
100 g/3½ oz chives
100 g/3½ oz dill
150 g/5 oz parsley
150 g/5 oz spinach
300 g/11 oz small turnips
1 teaspoon turmeric
1 litre/1¾ pints chicken or vegetable stock
juice of 1 lemon
30 g/1 oz butter
2 tablespoons vegetable oil
salt and pepper to taste

GARNISH

1 medium onion, finely chopped
4 tablespoons vegetable oil
1 teaspoon dried mint

GARNISH

Fry the onion in 2 tablespoons of oil until light brown. In another small frying pan, heat up 3 tablespoons of the oil and add the dried mint. Stir for half a minute and remove from the heat. Serve the *aash* in a soup bowl and decorate with both garnishes.

Mung bean soup is delicious with warm bread and pickles.

AABGUSHT

AABGUSHT, or lamb soup, is an old dish which traditionally, in caravanserai and tea houses, was cooked
and served in special clay pots called *deezi*, which have a
curved base suitable for placing on charcoal braziers to cook
slowly. In Iran *aabgusht is* often referred to as *deezi*.

The base soup is made from cuts from the neck or
shoulder of lamb, mixed with onion and pulses such as split
peas, chick peas and red kidney beans. It is seasoned with
lemon juice and flavoured with saffron. A wide variety of
herbs, fruits, tomato and potato can be added to this base,
creating a wonderful array of tastes and flavours.

Aabgusht can either be eaten as it is or it can be split into
two separate dishes. The broth can be strained off and served
as a soup, which is eaten with pieces of floating bread or
croutons. The remaining mix of meat and pulses is pounded.
Called *gusht kubideh*, it is eaten in warm flatbread with fresh
herbs, spring onions and pickles.

Aabgusht is a very easy dish to make, but it has to be
cooked slowly.

The following recipes are a selection from a wide variety
of *aabgushts*, each having a totally different flavour.

Original lamb soup

Aabgusht-e sadeh

SERVES 4–6
PREPARATION about 20
 minutes plus soaking
COOKING about 2¾ hours

INGREDIENTS

100 g/3½ oz split peas
4 shoulder shanks of lamb or
 1 kg/2¼ lb shoulder on the
 bone
1 large onion
3 medium potatoes
200 g/7 oz red kidney beans
 (canned)
2 teaspoons tomato purée
1 teaspoon turmeric
2 tablespoons vegetable oil
2 dried limes, washed, dried
 and pierced with a fork
 (*see* INGREDIENTS)
1½ litres/2½ pints hot water
2 tablespoons lemon juice
2 dessertspoons liquid saffron
 (*see* INGREDIENTS)
salt and pepper

My recipe is a variation on the traditional *aabgusht* as it contains potato and tomato purée. I prefer lamb shanks to the more fatty traditional cuts.

PREPARATION

Wash the lamb; with a sharp knife cut off any extra fat, tendon or skin from the shanks (or shoulder).

Wash the split peas and soak them in hot water for at least 30 minutes. Peel the onion and cut it into four sections. Wash, peel and cut the potatoes into four. Keep them in a bowl of water to avoid discolouration.

COOKING

Heat the oil in a medium-sized heavy-based saucepan (preferably cast iron) and toss the quartered onion in, cooking for a couple of minutes. Stir the lamb in with the onion and cook until the lamb is golden. Add the turmeric and stir so that the shanks are covered evenly. Drain the split peas and add to the pan. Add the dried limes. Pour the hot water into the pan and stir to mix the ingredients. Bring to the boil then lower the heat, put the lid on and let simmer gently until you are able to separate the meat from the bone with a fork and the split peas are al dente. This should take approximately 2 hours. If the liquid is reduced to less than two-thirds of the original, add more water: it is important that you end up with a thin broth.

Add the potatoes and tomato purée to the pan and stir to mix. Simmer very gently until the potatoes are cooked (30–35 minutes). Adjust the seasoning. Add the red kidney beans and continue to simmer for another 10 to 15 minutes. Add the lemon juice and simmer for a further five minutes. The consistency of the finished dish should resemble that of a soup not a stew. Before serving add 2 teaspoons of liquid saffron to the pan and mix.

As mentioned, *aabgusht* can be eaten as it is with warm flatbread such as pitta or *lavash*. Alternatively, the cooked meat and other ingredients can be pounded or mashed by hand or in a food processor and served separately; this is *gusht kubideh*. It can also be eaten cold as a sandwich filling, with pickles, herbs (*sabzi khordan*) and a side dish of cucumber yogurt.

Lamb soup with fruit

Aabgusht-e meeveh

SERVES 4–6
PREPARATION about 20
  minutes plus soaking
COOKING about 2 hours and
  30 minutes

INGREDIENTS

1 kg/2¼ lb lamb shoulder
    shanks or shoulder on the
    bone
100 g/3½ oz split peas
200 g/7 oz potato
1 large onion
3 dried limes
200 g/7 oz sour cooking apple
200 g/7 oz quince
100 g/3½ oz sour (morello)
    cherries (available frozen in
    some supermarkets)
100 g/3½ oz plums (any
    variety)
70 g/2½ oz dried apricots
70 g/2½ oz dried stoned
    prunes
1 teaspoon turmeric
4 dessertspoons liquid saffron
    (*see* INGREDIENTS)
1 teaspoon tomato purée
3 tablespoons lemon juice
3 tablespoons vegetable oil
salt and pepper
2½ litres/4 pints boiling water

GARNISH (OPTIONAL)

1 tablespoon dried mint
3 tablespoons vegetable oil

This delicious, exotic sweet-and-sour lamb soup is sometimes referred to as 'orchard' *aabgusht*, because of the variety of fruits that are used in it. In the north of Iran, where this soup is popular, it is made with seasonal fruits in summer, but in winter they use dried fruit or a mixture of dried and fresh winter fruits.

I prefer to make this soup with a mix of dried and fresh fruits. Dried fruits like prunes and apricots create a richer taste and give more body to the soup.

PREPARATION

Soak the split peas in hot water for at least 30–40 minutes. Wash the lamb and trim the excess fat. Peel the onion and cut it into 4–6 segments. Peel the apples, potatoes and quinces and cut them into 5 cm/2 inch chunks. Place them in a bowl with 1 teaspoon saffron liquid and 2 tablespoons lemon juice. Cut the apricots and prunes into 2 cm/¾ inch pieces and soak in warm water.

COOKING

In a large heavy-based saucepan, preferably cast iron, heat the oil; add the onion, the lamb, turmeric, dried limes, salt and pepper; stir and fry for a couple of minutes. Pour in the water, bring to the boil and then reduce the heat and simmer for an hour.

Drain the split peas, add to the pan and simmer for 30 minutes. The split peas should be soft when pressed with a spoon; if they are not, cook for a further 20–30 minutes. At this stage add the fruit mix, except for the cherries (if using). Add the potatoes and the tomato purée to the pan, stir well to mix all the ingredients. Add more water if you are left with less than two-thirds of the original volume. Simmer gently over a low heat for 30 minutes and then add the cherries (if using), the lemon juice and the saffron liquid; continue to cook for 10 more minutes.

For the garnish (if using), heat the oil in a small frying pan; when hot add the dried mint, stir and remove immediately.

Stir the soup well and pour into, preferably, a large clear glass bowl. Garnish with the mint mix.

This dish is delicious with warm flatbread and a side dish of *sabzi khordan* (fresh herbs).

Lamb soup with herbs and black-eyed beans

Aabgusht-e bozbaash

This is a nutritious, flavoursome soup. The herbs, combined with dried lime and cinnamon, give this dish layers of aroma and a wonderful fresh taste.

The soup used to be made with cuts from a young goat (hence the Persian name *bozbaash*), but nowadays cuts from neck or shoulder of lamb are used instead. I prefer to use shoulder shanks. My recipe also differs from the more traditional version in that I add coriander/cilantro and vegetable stock.

PREPARATION

Wash the lamb shanks and pat them dry with kitchen paper. Cut off any skin and excess fat with a sharp knife.

Wash the chives, parsley and coriander in cold water, discarding any tough stalks and wilting and yellowing leaves. Dry the leaves and tender stalks in a salad spinner or a clean tea towel. Finely chop the herbs using a sharp, wide-bladed knife.

Peel the onions; cut one into quarters and finely chop the other. Peel the potatoes and cut each into four pieces. Place the potato pieces in a bowl and cover with cold water to avoid discoloration.

COOKING

Heat 2 tablespoons of oil in a heavy-based saucepan, preferably cast iron, and toss the quartered onion in the oil for a couple of minutes. Add the lamb shanks and turn to seal on all sides. The meat should not be browned at this stage.

SERVES 4–6
PREPARATION about 30 minutes
COOKING about 2½ hours

INGREDIENTS

4 lamb shoulder shanks or 3 leg shanks (or 2 shanks and 2 neck cuts)
100 g/3½ oz chives
100 g/3½ oz coriander/cilantro
100 g/3½ oz parsley
2 tablespoons dried fenugreek
2 large onions
3 medium potatoes
4 tablespoons vegetable oil
2 teaspoons turmeric
2 dried limes, washed, dried and pierced with a fork (*see* INGREDIENTS)
1 cinnamon stick (5–10 cm/2–4 inches)
2 litres/3½ pints vegetable stock
salt and black pepper
200 g/7 oz canned black-eyed or red kidney beans (drained weight)
4 tablespoons lemon juice
2 dessertspoons liquid saffron (*see* INGREDIENTS)

GARNISH

1 medium onion, finely chopped
2 tablespoons vegetable oil
2 teaspoons liquid saffron

Add 1 teaspoon of the turmeric and stir to coat the shanks evenly. Pour the stock into the pan and stir well. Add the dried limes and the cinnamon stick. Bring back to the boil, then lower the heat and cover the pan with a lid. Allow to simmer gently for approximately 1½ hours until the shanks are nearly cooked (you should be able to separate the meat from the bone with a fork). Keep the heat low and keep the lid on the pan to retain as much of the liquid as possible. Add more water if necessary, to get back to soup consistency.

While the meat is cooking, heat the remaining oil in a large frying pan and fry the rest of the onion. Fold in the chopped fresh herbs and the fenugreek. Add 1 teaspoon of turmeric and fry gently for 5–10 minutes until the herbs shrink in volume and are well mixed with the onion. If the herbs start to stick to the pan, add another tablespoon of oil.

Stir the fried herb mixture and the potatoes into the lamb. Add the beans. Cover with a lid and simmer on a very low heat for 45 minutes. Taste and adjust the seasoning, add the lemon juice, and simmer for a further 5 minutes.

For the garnish, heat the oil in a frying pan and fry the chopped onion until golden brown; set to one side.

To serve, take the shanks and potato chunks out, stir the soup well, pour in to a large bowl, put the shanks back in and sprinkle the garnish and the liquid saffron all over.

Serve with warm flatbread such as pitta or *lavash* with a side dish of yogurt, pickles and fresh herbs (*sabzi khordan*).

ESHKENEH

ESHKENEHS (egg soups) are a speciality of the north, possibly because of Chinese influence. They are hardly ever made in the southern regions. There are many varieties of *eshkeneh*, ranging from simple fenugreek or coriander versions to more elaborate recipes made with quince, sour cherries or pomegranate syrup.

The base of *eshkeneh* is lightly fried onion mixed with fenugreek and other ingredients. Before serving, beaten or whole egg is added to the soup mix.

Original *eshkeneh*

Eshkeneh-e sadeh

SERVES 4–6
PREPARATION about 20
    minutes
COOKING about 45–50
    minutes

INGREDIENTS

1 medium onion
250 g/9 oz potatoes (any type)
50 g/2 oz celery
4 tablespoons dried fenugreek
30 g/1 oz fresh coriander/
    cilantro finely chopped
30 g/1 oz butter
1 teaspoon turmeric
juice of half a lemon
1 beaten egg
1 litre/1¾ pints stock

This is a light soup with a delicate but distinct fenugreek flavour. It is quick and easy to make and can be served as a starter or as a light lunch with flatbread.

My recipe is different from the traditional one, because I use celery, potato and coriander as well as fenugreek.

PREPARATION

Peel and finely chop the onion. Peel and dice the potatoes into ½ cm/¼ inch cubes. Wash and finely chop the celery sticks into 1 cm/½ inch pieces.

Wash the coriander and dry it, discard the tougher stalks and finely chop it with a sharp wide-bladed knife.

COOKING

Take a medium-sized heavy-based saucepan and melt the butter and oil together. When hot, fry the onion until golden. Add the potato, celery, coriander, fenugreek and turmeric to the fried onions. Stir well and sweat for a further 3 to 5 minutes on medium heat. Add the stock (vegetable stock if you want a vegetarian option) and let it simmer for 40 to 45 minutes on very low heat.

Before serving, and while the soup is simmering, whisk in the beaten egg, add the lemon juice and adjust seasoning to taste. Let it simmer, making sure it does not boil, for 5 more minutes. Serve in a soup bowl and garnish (optional) with finely sliced and crisply fried onions.

Eshkeneh is eaten with warm flatbread and a side dish of herbs (*sabzi khordan*) and spring onions.

This *eshkeneh* can be served as a starter with hot bread.

Pomegranate and fenugreek soup

Eshkeneh-e anaar

This is a light sweet-and-sour soup with a delicate but distinct fragrance of fenugreek and tangy pomegranate. It is quick and easy to make, with layers of flavour and aroma.

PREPARATION AND COOKING

Peel and finely chop the onion. Heat the butter and oil in a medium-sized heavy-based saucepan on a medium heat. Add the chopped onion, fry until golden; add the turmeric, fry for 1 minute then add the flour, mint and fenugreek; stir and fry for a couple of minutes and then add the vegetable stock. Bring to the boil, reduce the heat and add the pomegranate syrup and the sugar. Simmer for 30–40 minutes. Before serving beat the egg and whisk in. Let the soup simmer for 5 more minutes and then serve.

SERVES 4
PREPARATION AND
COOKING about 30–40
minutes

INGREDIENTS

1 medium-sized onion
1 teaspoon turmeric
1 tablespoon plain flour
2 dessertspoons caster sugar
800 ml/1½ pints vegetable
   stock
4 tablespoons dried mint
1 tablespoon dried fenugreek
200 ml/7 fl oz pomegranate
   syrup
1 egg
30 g/1 oz butter
2 tablespoons vegetable oil
salt and pepper to taste

Eshkeneh with walnuts and yogurt

Eshkeneh-e gherdoo va maast

This *eshkeneh* is a feast of flavours, combining the aroma of fenugreek and mint with the crunchiness of walnut, creamy yogurt and lemon juice.

I use celery and potato as the thickening base for the soup (*eshkeneh* is very thin, so these are not used traditionally).

PREPARATION

Peel and finely chop the onion and the garlic. Peel the potato and dice it into small cubes. Wash and finely chop the celery.

COOKING

In a heavy-based saucepan, melt the butter and 2 tablespoons of the oil and fry the onion until golden. Add the garlic, stir-fry for a couple of minutes and then add the chopped celery and potato, fenugreek, half of the lemon juice, and salt and pepper to taste. Reduce the heat and allow the mix to sweat for approximately 5 minutes. Add the stock and simmer until the potato and celery are cooked, approximately 40 minutes. Add the walnuts and simmer for a further 10 minutes, adding water if the consistency is too thick. Beat the egg and add to the pan, stirring vigorously to blend the egg in. Cook for a further 5 minutes, making sure it does not boil. Remove from the heat and fold in the yogurt. Stir well to a smooth mix. Add the rest of the lemon juice and adjust seasoning. Keep warm.

In a small frying pan heat the remaining oil and stir in the mint, remove from the heat, add to the main pan, stir to mix well. Serve in a bowl.

This is a wonderful vegetarian starter but can be eaten with garlic bread as a light meal.

SERVES 4

PREPARATION AND
  COOKING about 50–55
  minutes

INGREDIENTS

1 large onion
3 cloves of garlic
2–3 celery sticks
1 large potato
2 tablespoons dried fenugreek
  leaves
1 tablespoon dried mint
50 g/2 oz crushed walnut
  pieces
1 egg
4 tablespoons Greek-style
  yogurt
Juice of 1 large lemon
750 ml/1¼ pints vegetable
  stock
30 g/1 oz butter
4 tablespoons vegetable oil

Almond soup

Harireh baadaam

SERVES 4
PREPARATION AND
   COOKING about 50 minutes

INGREDIENTS
200 g/7 oz ground almonds
1 dessertspoon rice flour
1 small onion
500 ml/1 pint vegetable stock
250 ml/½ pint milk
zest and juice of half an
   unwaxed lemon
30 g/1 oz butter
salt

Literally translated, the name means 'chiffon-like almonds', referring to the lightness of the dish's texture. *Harireh* is traditionally made not with milk but with the milk-like juice extracted from adding water to pounded almonds and passing the mixture through muslin. But I use milk in my recipe.

Almond soup can also be made with sugar and served as a sweet.

PREPARATION

Peel and very finely chop the onion.

You can use either ready-made ground almonds or grind skinned almonds in a food processor to release their subtle aroma.

COOKING

In a medium-sized pan melt the butter, fry the onions until golden; add the ground almonds and stir for 1 minute. Add the rice flour to the almonds and stir thoroughly for a couple of minutes until completely mixed. Gradually add the stock and continue to stir to obtain the smooth consistency of a thick soup. Add the milk and simmer gently on low heat for 30–40 minutes. Before serving, add the zest and the juice of the lemon and adjust the seasoning. (For a smoother consistency you can sieve the soup.) Fried onions can be added as a garnish.

TIP I have cooked both sweet and savoury *harireh* a number of times. The soup made with stock and milk remains my preferred version.

CHAPTER 3

Khoreshes

KHORESH, or *khoresht*, is an essential component of
Persian cuisine. In Persian *khoresh* means meal, an
indication of its centrality. It is possible to do without rice
and replace it with bread, but *khoresh* itself is irreplaceable.
Khoresh, basically, is a rich sauce made from meat, chicken
or fish combined with vegetables, herbs, fruits or pulses.
Khoresh is usually served with plain rice (*chelo*), but can also
be eaten with bread.

The ingredients in a *khoresh* change depending on
seasonal availability. There are numerous varieties of
khoresh, and each region of Iran puts its own stamp on the
dish. In the lush parts in the north of the country fruits and
herbs are the dominant ingredients; these *khoreshes* are more
sweet-and-sour in flavour. Those from the south contain
more pulses or vegetables and are distinctly spicy. In the
north *khoreshes* are expected to be thinner and more juicy,
whereas in the south a well-cooked *khoresh* is allowed to
simmer longer and is therefore thicker.

Basics of cooking *khoresh*

All recipes for *khoresh* follow the same general rule. You
almost always cook the meat initially the same way before
introducing other ingredients. Depending on the recipe,
chop 1 or 2 onions and fry them in oil until golden. Add the
meat and seal all around so the edges change colour and the
tips go slightly brown.

Khoresh-e seeb

The meat traditionally used in Persian cooking is lamb; the leg bone is added for more flavour. In some *khoreshes* lamb can be replaced with chicken or fish.

Most *khoreshes* can be made without meat; they make a wonderful balanced vegetarian dishes because they contain so many ingredients.

Apple *khoresh*

Khoresh-e seeb

The north-eastern province of Khorasan is famous for its fruit orchards. A wide variety of apples are grown there, from small aromatic ones known as *golaab* apple (rose apple) to the very sour variety known as *seeb-e torsh*.

Apples are used widely in Persian cuisine, particularly in jams, pickles and many dishes, including *aabgushts* (lamb soups) and *khoreshes*.

This sweet-and-sour apple *khoresh* can be made with lamb or chicken.

The apple used for this dish should be firm and tangy, as it must not disintegrate during cooking.

PREPARATION

Wash and peel the apples; cut them into halves and remove the core and seeds, then cut each half lengthwise into approximately 4 cm/1½ inch pieces.

Peel and chop the onion. Trim the lamb and remove any extra fat, dice into small (1 cm/½ inch) cubes; wash and dry thoroughly. Sprinkle with salt and a small amount of black pepper.

COOKING

In a medium-sized pan, fry the onions in 2 tablespoons of vegetable oil until golden. Add the lamb pieces and fry them for about 5 minutes until lightly brown. Add the turmeric, 2 teaspoons of liquid saffron and the tomato purée, stir and then add 300 ml/10 fl oz boiling water. Add 2 tablespoons of sugar, stir to dissolve and bring to the boil. Reduce the heat and simmer for about 45–50 minutes. The meat should be fully cooked by this stage.

SERVES 4
PREPARATION about 15 minutes
COOKING about 1 hour and 10 minutes

INGREDIENTS

500 g/1 lb 2 oz apples (Bramley or Cox)
500 g/1 lb 2 oz boned leg of lamb
1 medium onion
4 tablespoons vegetable oil
20 g/¾ oz butter
1 teaspoon turmeric
2 dessertspoons liquid saffron (*see* INGREDIENTS)
3 tablespoons sugar
juice of 1 large lemon (3 tablespoons lemon juice)
1 dessertspoon tomato purée
salt and black pepper to taste

Whilst the meat is cooking, melt the butter and 2 tablespoon of sugar together in a heavy-based saucepan; arrange the apple pieces in the frying pan and caramelise.

Add the rest of the saffron, and the rest of the lemon juice.

Add the caramelised apples to the pan and simmer for 10–15 minutes. The apple pieces should not disintegrate. Check the seasoning and adjust to taste.

Serve the *khoresh* in a shallow bowl, taking care not to break the apple pieces.

This dish goes well with plain rice and a side dish of fresh herbs and/or a green salad with citrus dressing.

Aubergine and herb *khoresh*

Naaz khatoon

Aubergine is very popular all over Iran. Lamb and aubergine *khoresh* is commonly made with tomatoes and tomato purée with split peas (*ghiemeh badenjan*) or without (*khoresh-e badenjan*, which featured in *New Persian Cooking*). In this dish from the north (Caspian seashore), mint and parsley form the base of the *khoresh*, combined with aubergine and seasoned with sour grape juice (verjuice), which is delicious and aromatic. *Naaz khatoon* can also be cooked with eggs in place of meat as a vegetarian main course.

PREPARATION

Peel the aubergines, sprinkle with salt and let them sweat for around 15 minutes. Wash and dry them on paper kitchen towel.

Remove any excess fat from the lean meat and dice into 1 cm/½ inch cubes. Peel and finely chop the onions.

Wash and dry the herbs in a salad crisper. Discard the tough stems. With a sharp wide-bladed knife chop the herbs finely.

COOKING

In a medium-sized (25 cm/10 inches in diameter) saucepan fry half of the chopped onion in 2 tablespoons of oil until golden. Add the diced lamb, 1 teaspoon turmeric and salt and pepper to taste. Stir until the meat is well covered with the turmeric and sealed all over. Add the water, bring to boil, then turn the heat down and simmer for about 45 minutes to 1 hour until the meat is cooked.

SERVES 4
PREPARATION about 30–35 minutes
COOKING about 1½ hours

INGREDIENTS

400 g/14 oz lean leg of lamb
8 baby aubergines
150 g/5 oz parsley
120 g/4 oz mint
2 medium onions
1 teaspoon turmeric
2 dessertspoons liquid saffron (*see* INGREDIENTS)
100 ml/3½ fl oz vegetable oil
juice of 1 large lemon or 2 tablespoons sour grape juice
500 ml/1 pint boiling water

Whilst the meat is cooking, fry the baby aubergines in 3 tablespoons of oil (add more oil if needed as aubergines absorb a lot). Remove when golden and place on paper kitchen towel to remove extra oil.

In the same frying pan, add 2 tablespoons of the oil and fry the rest of the onions until golden, add 1 teaspoon turmeric, fry for 1 minute and then add the chopped herbs. Fry for 3–5 minutes; set to one side.

Add the herbs to the meat and allow to simmer for 20–25 minutes. At this stage there should be little liquid left as this *khoresh* is quite thick, so reduce the sauce further if needed. Add the aubergines, lemon juice and half of the saffron liquid and cook gently for 10 minutes.

Remove from the heat and let the pan stand for 10 minutes before serving.

Serve in a shallow dish. Take the aubergines out very carefully (making sure not to break them) and arrange the herb sauce around them. Sprinkle the rest of the saffron over the aubergines.

Naaz khatoon is served with plain rice. A side dish of yogurt and cucumber (*maast va khiar*, p. 190) goes well with this dish.

Chicken and yellow prune *khoresh*

Khoresh-e aaloo Bokhara

This is a comfort food for me, reminding me of my childhood in Shiraz. I remember coming back from school for lunch, entering the house and smelling the aroma of this dish. Cooking it now for my family evokes happy memories of cold but sunny winter days at home, as this dish was usually cooked in winter.

Aaloo Bokhara is a small dried yellow prune available from Persian or Middle Eastern shops. It is tangier and more flavoursome than the dried black prune.

PREPARATION

Peel and chop the onion. Soak the prunes in a bowl of boiling water to soften them (approximately 20 minutes).

Peel the potatoes, cut them lengthwise into halves and keep in cold water.

Wash the chicken fillets, trim off any fat and dry them.

COOKING

In a heavy-based saucepan fry the onion in the cooking oil until golden, add 1 teaspoon of turmeric and the chicken thighs. Fry to seal the chicken thighs. Add the tomato purée, salt and pepper, stir and add the stock. Reduce the heat, cover and allow to simmer. After 20 minutes, drain the potatoes and add to the pan.

Continue cooking for another 20 minutes. At this stage the chicken pieces and potatoes are soft and the sauce should have been reduced to almost half of the original volume. Drain the prunes and add them to the pan with the lemon juice, sugar and saffron liquid. Simmer covered for a further

SERVES 4
PREPARATION about 10 minutes plus soaking
COOKING about 1 hour

INGREDIENTS

6 skinless chicken thigh fillets
300 g/11 oz *aaloo Bokhara* (dried yellow prunes)
300 g/11 oz salad potatoes
1 medium onion
1 teaspoon turmeric
2 dessertspoons tomato purée
juice of 1 large lemon
2 tablespoons sugar
2 dessertspoons saffron
4 tablespoons vegetable oil
300 ml/1 pint chicken stock
salt and pepper

20 minutes. Check the seasoning; add more lemon juice or sugar depending on your taste.

Serve the *khoresh* in a shallow bowl with plain rice and a side dish of green salad and/or herbs (*sabzi khordan*).

Khoresh-e aaloo Bokhara

Chicken and Seville orange *khoresh*

Khoresh-e naaranj

Citrus fruits have been grown in the Caspian region and in the southern province of Fars for thousands of years. However, the sweet oranges called *Portoghal* were only brought to Iran by the Portuguese in the sixteenth century, hence the name. The original sour oranges, equivalent to Seville oranges, are called *naaranj*. Citrus fruits are used widely in Persian cooking all over the country.

Naaranj or Seville oranges are more aromatic and flavoursome than sweet oranges and therefore more suitable for this *khoresh*, although sweet oranges can be used too.

PREPARATION

Wash the chicken pieces, trim off any fat and dry them.

Peel and finely chop the onion.

Using a vegetable peeler, peel 3 oranges thinly (leaving behind as much of the white pith as possible) and cut the peels into juliennes. Separate the peeled oranges into segments and with a sharp knife remove the pith from each segment. Peel the carrots and cut them into juliennes as well. Squeeze the fourth orange for juice.

COOKING

Put the Seville orange juliennes in a small pan of cold water, bring to the boil and drain in a strainer; refresh under cold running water, test for bitterness and if needed repeat the process until the juliennes are no longer bitter. Set to one side.

Heat the oil in a medium-sized saucepan and fry the onion to golden, add the chicken pieces and fry to seal them (about

SERVES 4
PREPARATION about 30 minutes
COOKING 1 hour and 20 minutes

INGREDIENTS

8 skinless chicken pieces (legs and breasts)
4 Seville oranges
3 large carrots
1 medium onion
1 teaspoon turmeric
1 teaspoon tomato purée
2 tablespoons liquid saffron (*see* INGREDIENTS)
3 dessertspoons sugar
30 g/1 oz butter
3 tablespoons vegetable oil
500 ml/1 pint chicken stock
salt and pepper

GARNISH (OPTIONAL)

20 g pistachio slivers
20 g flaked almonds (almond slivers)
1 tablespoon vegetable oil

8–10 minutes). Add the turmeric, salt and pepper and tomato purée, and stir well. Now add the chicken stock, bring to boil, reduce the heat, cover and simmer for 30–40 minutes. The chicken pieces should be soft and the sauce reduced to almost a third.

Whilst the chicken is cooking, melt the butter with a tablespoon of oil and a dessertspoon of sugar in a heavy-based frying pan and fry the carrot juliennes on medium heat for about 10 minutes; they should be glistening, golden – make sure not to brown them. Add the orange juliennes, stir-fry for a couple of minutes, add 2 teaspoons of liquid saffron and set to one side.

Fold in the carrot and orange mix into the chicken and allow to simmer for 15 minutes. Before serving, add the orange segments, the juice of the Seville orange, the rest of the sugar and the liquid saffron, simmer for a further 5 minutes or so, but not for too long as the orange juliennes will disintegrate.

For the garnish, heat the oil in a small frying pan and stir-fry the almond and pistachio slivers for a minute.

Serve in a shallow bowl; take the chicken pieces out first, pour the sauce over them and add the garnish on top.

This is a dish with an array of aromas and flavours; a plain dish of rice and a plate of herbs (*sabzi khordan*) go very well with it.

Mint and parsley *khoresh*

Khoresh-e naana Jaffary

SERVES 4–6
PREPARATION 30 minutes
COOKING about 1¾ hours

INGREDIENTS

400 g/14 oz stewing lamb or
    veal
120 g/4 oz fresh mint
350 g/12 oz flat leaf parsley
350 g/12 oz yellow prunes
    (*aaloo Bokhara*) or dried
    pitted prunes
1 medium onion
1 small onion
50 g/2 oz butter
8 tablespoons vegetable oil
2 teaspoons turmeric
salt and black pepper
600 ml/1 pt boiling water
100 ml/3½ fl oz lemon juice
2 tablespoons sugar
4 dessertspoons liquid saffron
    (*see* INGREDIENTS)

The combination of mint and parsley is deliciously aromatic and the sweet-and-sour taste of yellow prunes adds an extra level of flavour. The lemon juice mixed with sugar and saffron intensifies the sweet-and-sour with a delicate, piquant edge.

PREPARATION

Wash the herbs and dry them in a salad spinner. Cut off and discard any tough stalks; chop the leaves finely with a sharp wide-bladed knife.

Wash the lamb or veal and dry on paper kitchen towel. Trim off any skin and fat, and cut the meat into 3–4 cm/1½ inch cubes.

Peel and chop both onions, keeping them separate.

Soak the prunes in a cup of hot water mixed with 2 teaspoons liquid saffron and 2 tablespoons lemon juice.

COOKING

Heat 30 g/1 oz of the butter with 4 tablespoons of the oil in a medium-sized heavy-based saucepan. Fry the chopped medium onion until golden.

Add the meat and 1 teaspoon of the turmeric, season with salt and pepper. Stir to brown the meat lightly on all sides.

Add the hot water and reduce the heat. Cover with a lid and simmer on a low heat for about an hour or until the meat is cooked: it should be tender enough to cut with a fork.

While the meat is cooking, fry the chopped small onion in the remaining 4 tablespoons of oil in a frying pan/skillet until golden brown. Add the herbs and fry for 5 minutes until the herb mixture has reduced in volume and is mixed with the fried onions. Add the remaining 1 teaspoon of turmeric, plus salt and pepper to taste.

Stir the herb mixture into the meat sauce, which should have reduced to almost half its original volume (about 400 ml). Add the prunes, lemon juice, half of the saffron and sugar. Cover and simmer gently for another 30 minutes, or until the sauce is thickened.

Add the remaining butter and mix well. The *khoresh* should have a subtle sweet-and-sour taste. Serve in a shallow bowl, sprinkling the remaining saffron on top.

Like any other *khoresh*, this recipe is eaten with a dish of plain rice (*chelo*). A side dish of mixed salad and/or a plate of *sabzi khordan* (fresh herbs) is ideal with it.

Pumpkin *khoresh*

Khoresh-e kadoo halvai

In Iran pumpkin is used to make jam and halva (a sweet aromatic dessert), hence the name *halvai*, which means a vegetable suitable for making halva.

Pumpkin *khoresh* is an aromatic sweet-and-sour dish. The combination of caramelised pumpkin with a touch of tomato purée, saffron, cinnamon and lemon juice creates an aesthetically pleasing and flavoursome dish.

In the north this is also made as a vegetarian dish (recipe below) with walnut and pomegranate juice.

PREPARATION

Wash the meat, trim off any skin or fat and cut into 4–5 cm/2 inch cubes. Cut the pumpkin, remove the seeds; skin and cut into chunky 8 cm/3 inch cubes. Peel and chop the onion.

COOKING

In a medium-sized heavy-based saucepan heat half of the oil and fry the onion until golden. Add the meat cubes, turmeric tomato purée, salt and pepper, stir well, fry for a couple of minutes until the meat is golden, and then add the boiling water. Reduce the heat, cover and simmer on a low heat until the meat is tender, approximately 1½ hours. The juice should be half the original volume at this stage.

Whilst the meat is cooking, caramelise the pumpkin cubes. In a large frying pan, melt the butter with rest of the oil and 2 tablespoons of sugar. Add the pumpkin cubes and cook on a low heat until golden brown and caramelised (around 10–15 minutes).

SERVES 4
PREPARATION about 15 minutes
COOKING about 2 hours

INGREDIENTS

500 g/1 lb 2 oz lean leg of lamb
500 g/1 lb 2 oz pumpkin
1 medium onion
1 teaspoon turmeric
1 cinnamon stick
2 tablespoons liquid saffron
   (*see* INGREDIENTS)
3 tablespoons lemon juice
4 dessertspoons sugar
4 tablespoons vegetable oil
30 g/1 oz butter
1 tablespoon tomato purée
1 litre/1¾ pints boiling water
salt and pepper to taste

Add to the pan the caramelised pumpkin, the cinnamon stick, saffron, the lemon juice and the remaining sugar, stir with care so as not to break up the pumpkin. Simmer for a further 30 minutes until the pumpkin is just soft. Make sure not to overcook as the pumpkin cubes should stay whole and not disintegrate. Check the seasoning: you might need to add more sugar or lemon juice depending on your taste for sweet-and-sourness.

Place in a large shallow dish, arrange the pumpkin cubes on top. Serve with plain rice (*chelo*) and a side dish of herbs (*sabzi khordan*) or a green salad.

Vegetarian pumpkin *khoresh*

In the north, in the province of Gilan by the Caspian Sea, they make pumpkin *khoresh* with walnut and pomegranate syrup, without meat.

PREPARATION

Cut the pumpkin, remove the seeds; skin and cut into chunky 8 cm/3 inch cubes. Peel and chop the onion.

COOKING

Heat the oil in a medium-sized heavy-based pan and fry the onions to golden; add the ground walnuts, stir well for a couple of minutes, add the vegetable stock, pomegranate syrup and the sugar; reduce the heat, cover and simmer gently.

Caramelise the pumpkins, as described in the previous recipe, add the *golpar*, stir to coat the pumpkins, add to the pan. Simmer half-covered for a further 20–30 minutes. Before serving add the liquid saffron; check the seasoning. The sauce should be black and quite thick in consistency.

SERVES 4
PREPARATION about 15 minutes
COOKING about 45 minutes

INGREDIENTS

500 g/1 lb 2 oz cubed pumpkin
1 medium onion, peeled and finely chopped
½ teaspoon turmeric
1 teaspoon *golpar* (see INGREDIENTS)
500 ml/1 pint vegetable stock
200 g/7 oz ground walnuts
350 ml/12 fl oz pomegranate syrup
2 dessertspoons sugar
2 tablespoons liquid saffron (*see* INGREDIENTS)
30 g/1 oz butter
3 tablespoons vegetable oil

Quince and chicken *khoresh*

Khoresh-e beh

SERVES 4
PREPARATION about 15
   minutes
COOKING about 1 hour

INGREDIENTS

2 medium quinces
1 medium onion
6 skinless chicken thighs
3 tablespoons vegetable oil
20 g/¾ oz butter
1 teaspoon turmeric
2 tablespoons liquid saffron
   (*see* INGREDIENTS)
4 tablespoons sugar
juice of 1 large lemon (about
   3 tablespoons lemon juice)
250 ml/9 fl oz chicken stock
1 tablespoon tomato purée
salt and black pepper to taste
30 g/1 oz flaked almonds to
   garnish (optional)

Quince is a favourite fruit for making jam. It is also used to make this delicious sweet-and-sour *khoresh*.

PREPARATION

Wash and peel the quinces; halve them and remove the seeds, then cut each half lengthwise into approximately 2 cm/¾ inch-thick pieces.

Peel and chop the onion. Trim the chicken thighs; wash and dry them thoroughly. Sprinkle with salt and a small amount of black pepper.

COOKING

In a medium-sized pan, fry the onions in 2 tablespoons of vegetable oil until golden, then add the turmeric. Add the chicken pieces and fry them for about 5 minutes until lightly golden on both sides. Add 2 teaspoons of liquid saffron and the tomato purée, stir and then add the stock, half of the lemon juice and 2 tablespoons of sugar; stir and bring to boil. Reduce the heat and simmer for about 30 minutes.

Whilst the chicken is cooking, caramelise the quince pieces in the butter and the rest of the oil, adding the rest of the saffron, 2 tablespoons of sugar and rest of the lemon juice.

Add the caramelised quince to the pan, stir gently and simmer for 10–15 minutes. Adjust the seasoning. If the garnish is to be used, before serving roast the almond flakes lightly in a small frying pan. Serve the *khoresh* in a shallow bowl; pour the almond flakes on top. It is ideal with plain rice (*chelo*) and a plate of fresh herbs (*sabzi khordan*) or a green salad.

Rhubarb *khoresh*

Khoresh-e reevas

The tartness of rhubarb combined with parsley and mint create layers of pleasing taste and aroma in this dish.

In Britain rhubarb crumble and rhubarb fool are very popular desserts; savoury rhubarb dishes are less common. Preparing the herbs takes time but it is worth it; this can be done whilst the meat is cooking.

PREPARATION AND COOKING

Wash the lamb and dry it on paper kitchen towel. Cut off any fat and skin and dice the meat into 2 cm/1 inch cubes. Fry half of the chopped onions in half of the cooking oil until golden. Add the meat cubes and turmeric and stir well to seal and cover the meat in oil and turmeric. Add salt and pepper; once the meat has browned, add the vegetable stock. Bring to the boil and reduce the heat. Allow to simmer until the meat is cooked well enough that it can be easily pierced with a fork. This should take 1 hour for good-quality lamb.

Whilst the lamb is cooking, prepare the herbs and the rhubarb. Wash the herbs and dry them in a salad crisper or a clean tea towel. Discard any wilting or yellow leaves and tough stalks. Chop them finely with a sharp wide-bladed knife. Wash the rhubarb stems and dry them. Cut them into 3–4 cm/1½ inch chunks.

Using a deep frying pan big enough to hold the herbs, fry the rest of the onions in the rest of the oil, until golden. Add the chopped herbs and fry gently for five minutes. The herbs will shrink alarmingly, but don't worry – the flavours are all captured. With a slotted spoon take the fried herbs and add them to the meat, stir well and allow to simmer for

SERVES 4–6
PREPARATION about 30 minutes
COOKING about 1½ hours

INGREDIENTS

500 g/1 lb 2 oz lean lamb (fillet or leg)
350 g/12 oz young rhubarb stems (make sure you throw away the leaves carefully as they are poisonous to animals)
250 g/9 oz parsley
100 g/3½ oz mint
2 medium onions
1 teaspoon turmeric
50 g/2 oz butter
100 ml/3½ fl oz vegetable oil
350 ml/12 fl oz hot vegetable stock

15 minutes until the herbs are cooked and the aroma is well developed. In the same frying pan stir-fry the rhubarb stems for 1 minute. Add the rhubarb to the herb-and-meat mix and simmer for 10 minutes. Rhubarb cooks very quickly and can disintegrate; make sure not to overcook it.

At the end of this period the sauce should be thick with the herbs; adjust the seasoning to taste before serving. If you like a more tangy taste, add some lemon juice.

Serve with plain rice and a side dish of yogurt.

Khoresh-e reevas

Chicken and potato curry *khoresh*

Khoresh-e morgh va seebzamini ba curry

Curry-spiced potato dishes are very popular in the south of Iran. Combined with meat, chicken or vegetables they make delicious *khoraks* or *khoreshes*.

This *khoresh* is a Bushehri version of Indian chicken curry which is modified to Persian taste.

PREPARATION

Peel and finely chop the onions. Chop the chilli. Peel the garlic cloves and crush them in a pestle and mortar with the chopped chilli. Peel the potatoes and cut them in half lengthwise.

COOKING

In a heavy-based saucepan melt half of the butter with half of the oil and fry the chicken pieces to seal on all sides (approximately 8–10 minutes). Take them out with a slotted spoon and keep warm. Add the rest of the butter and oil to the same pan and fry the onions until golden and then add the ginger and the garlic and chilli paste; stir fry for a couple of minutes. Return the chicken to the pan, add the turmeric, curry powder and tomato purée; stir to mix well so that all the chicken pieces are well coated. Pour the stock into the pan, stir and bring to the boil, reduce the heat and simmer for 20 minutes and then add the potatoes.

Cook for a further 30 minutes until the chicken pieces and potatoes are cooked. The potatoes should not disintegrate. The sauce should be quite thick at this stage; if it is not, take the chicken out and further reduce the sauce. Add the lemon juice and adjust the seasoning before serving.

Serve with plain rice and a yogurt dish and a side plate of fresh herbs (*sabzi khordan*).

SERVES 4
PREPARATION about 15 minutes
COOKING about 1 hour

INGREDIENTS

2 skinless chicken breasts
2 skinless chicken thighs
1 medium onion
6 cloves of garlic
300 g/11 oz salad potatoes
1 teaspoon turmeric
1 hot green chilli
1 teaspoon grated fresh ginger
1 tablespoon curry powder
1 tablespoon tomato purée
500 ml/1 pint chicken stock
juice of 1 large lemon
30 g/1 oz butter
4 tablespoons vegetable oil
salt and pepper to taste

Red lentil daal

Daal adas-e Bushehri

Indian *daal* is well known and popular in the West. This version, from Bushehr on the Persian Gulf, is different because curry spices are not used, and because potato, tomato purée and lemon juice are added to the dish.

This is a delicious, nutritious vegetarian meal, quick and easy to cook; you can serve it with plain rice or flatbread.

PREPARATION

Wash the lentils and drain. Peel and finely chop the onion. Chop the chillies and crush them with the peeled garlic cloves in a pestle and mortar. Peel the potatoes and cut them in half.

COOKING

In a heavy-based saucepan, heat the oil and fry the onions until translucent, add the crushed garlic and chillies and the turmeric; stir and fry for a couple of minutes. Add the lentil and the potatoes, stir, then add the tomato purée; mix well by stirring rapidly. Pour the stock into the pan, stir, and bring to the boil; reduce the heat, cover and allow to simmer for approximately 45 minutes. Before serving adjust seasoning.

Daal is usually served with warm bread (or garlic bread) and chilli pickles, but it is equally delicious with plain rice and a side dish of tomato and onion salad.

SERVES 4
PREPARATION about 10 minutes
COOKING about 40–45 minutes

INGREDIENTS
120 g/4 oz red lentils
120 g/4 oz potatoes (preferably salad potatoes)
1 medium onion
1 teaspoon turmeric
6 cloves of garlic
1 or 2 hot chillies (depending on taste)
1 tablespoon tomato purée
600 ml/1 pint vegetable stock
3 tablespoons lemon juice
3 tablespoons vegetable oil
salt and pepper

Khoresh-e morgh va seebzamini ba curry

Spicy coriander *khoresh*

Khoresh-e aaloo gashneez

This is a wonderfully aromatic and spicy *khoresh* combining fragrant coriander, chilli and garlic with lamb and potato. It is a southern variation on a most popular and famous *khoresh*, *ghormeh sabzi* (lamb with red kidney beans and herbs, the recipe for which can be found in *New Persian Cooking*). In the south they refer to 'potato' as 'prune', or in Persian *aaloo*, hence the name *aaloo gashneez*.

PREPARATION

Wash the lamb, pat dry and trim off any skin and fat. Cut the meat into 4–5 cm/2 inch cubes.

Peel and finely chop – separately – the onions, chilli and garlic. Wash and dry the whole dried limes and pierce each a couple of times with a fork.

Wash the coriander in cold water, discarding any tough stalks and wilting or yellowing leaves. Dry the leaves and tender stalks in a salad spinner or a clean tea towel. Chop the coriander using a sharp wide-bladed knife.

Peel the potatoes, cut them in half and keep in cold water to prevent darkening.

COOKING

Heat 2 tablespoons of the oil in a medium-sized heavy-based saucepan. Fry half of the chopped onions until golden (approximately 10 minutes).

Add the lamb, 1 teaspoon of turmeric, half of the chopped garlic and 2 of the dried limes. Mix thoroughly and fry the meat until lightly brown and sealed on all sides.

SERVES 4
PREPARATION about 20–25 minutes
COOKING about 2 hours

INGREDIENTS

500 g/1 lb 2 oz lean leg of lamb
300 g/11 oz salad potatoes
2 medium onions
500 g/1 lb 2 oz fresh coriander/ cilantro
5 cloves of garlic
1 hot chilli (more if you prefer it spicier)
5 dried limes
1 dessertspoon powdered dry lime (can be obtained from Persian or Middle Eastern shops)
1 teaspoon turmeric
4 tablespoons vegetable oil
1 litre/1¾ pints boiling water
2 tablespoons lemon juice
salt and pepper

Daal adas-e Bushehri

Add the hot water, bring to boil then reduce the heat to low and cover and allow to simmer for 1 hour or until the meat is nearly cooked: it should be tender enough to cut with a fork. You should have about 500 ml/a pint of liquid left in the pan. If necessary, remove the meat to a plate and continue to simmer and reduce the stock further.

Meanwhile, heat the remaining oil in a large frying pan and fry the rest of the onion. Add the rest of the garlic, the chilli and 1 teaspoon of turmeric, and stir well. Fold in the chopped coriander. Add the powdered lime and fry gently for 5–10 minutes until the herbs shrink in volume and are well mixed with the onion, garlic and chilli. If the herbs start to stick to the pan, add another tablespoon of oil.

Add the fried coriander to the meat pan with the rest of the dried limes. Cover with a lid and simmer on a very low heat for 40 minutes. The potatoes should be soft at this stage; simmer more if they are still tough – make sure they stay whole. Taste and adjust the seasoning, adding lemon juice, salt and pepper and simmer for a further 5 minutes.

Take the pan off the heat and leave to stand for 15–20 minutes before serving, or as long as 45 minutes if you have time, so the flavours can develop more.

Serve in a shallow bowl, accompanied by plain rice and a tomato and onion salad.

Spicy fish *khoresh* with coconut milk

Khoresh-e mahi ba naarghil

The coastal regions by the Persian Gulf are famous for their variety of fish dishes. A wide range of fish and styles of cooking are utilised, from roasting in clay ovens to grilling on charcoal and frying.

In Bushehr, this *khoresh* is made with *halva* fish, which is a small flat fish with a shiny skin. The dish is equally good with any firm white fish fillet, such as cod. My recipe is slightly different from the original: I add coconut milk, which gives it an extra flavour and a creamy consistency. This is a delicious dish, easy to prepare and cook.

PREPARATION

Peel the onion and chop finely. Peel the garlic; chop the chillies coarsely. In a pestle and mortar crush the garlic and chillies together. Grate the fresh ginger.

Wash the fillets and pat dry, sprinkle with salt and pepper, place in a flat dish and squeeze half of a lemon over them.

COOKING

In a heavy-based saucepan, melt the butter with the oil and fry the onions to golden; add the ginger, crushed garlic and chilli mix and stir-fry for a couple of minutes. Reduce the heat and then add the tomato purée and the fish stock; stir well. Pour the coconut milk into the pan, stir and allow to simmer for 20–25 minutes so that the sauce thickens. Add the fish fillets and the lemon juice and cook for just 5–10 minutes, make sure that the fillets do not disintegrate.

This *khoresh* is delicious with plain rice; in the south it is sometimes eaten with *dami* (sticky rice). Coriander chutney (*chutni-e gashneez*, p. 201) goes well on the side.

SERVES 4
PREPARATION about 10 minutes
COOKING about 35–40 minutes

INGREDIENTS

500 g/1 lb 2 oz cod fillet (or any firm white fish)
1 large onion
5 cloves of garlic
1 tablespoon tomato purée
1 teaspoon turmeric
1 teaspoon fresh ginger
1 red chilli
1 green chilli
250 ml/9 fl oz fish stock
2 tablespoons vegetable oil
30 g/1 oz butter
300 ml/10 fl oz coconut milk
juice of 1½ lemons
salt and pepper

Spicy prawn *khoresh*

Khoresh-e maygoo

SERVES 4
PREPARATION
   about 10 minutes
COOKING about
   35–40 minutes

INGREDIENTS

500 g/1 lb 2 oz raw peeled
   prawns
1 medium onion
5–6 cloves of garlic
1 green chilli
1 red chilli
1 teaspoon fresh ginger
1 teaspoon ground cumin
1 teaspoon ground coriander
   seed
1 teaspoon turmeric
1 teaspoon tomato purée
juice of 1 lemon
3 tablespoons vegetable oil
250 ml/9 fl oz fish stock

Prawns are used in many recipes from the southern regions on the Persian Gulf.

This *khoresh* is greatly influenced by Indian prawn curry, but different spices are used. The Indian version is spicier and hotter, as they use more chillies and combine many more spices together.

PREPARATION

Peel and finely chop the onion. Grate the fresh ginger. Chop the chillies. In a pestle and mortar crush the garlic with the chopped chillies; mix with the coriander, turmeric and cumin.

If necessary, devein the prawns by cutting along the back and removing the black vein.

COOKING

In a saucepan, heat the oil and fry the onion to golden. Add the ginger, stir-fry for a minute and then add the crushed garlic, chilli and spices mix. Fry for a couple of minutes. Add the tomato purée followed by the fish stock, stir well, bring to the boil and reduce the heat. Simmer for 30 minutes or more, until the sauce is thickened. Add the prawns and the lemon juice, and cook for just 4–5 minutes – take care not to overcook the prawns as they tend to go leathery. Check the seasoning and stir well before serving. This dish is ideal with plain rice, a hot chutney and any green leaf salad.

CHAPTER 4

Khoraks

KHORAK in Farsi means food, and refers to a variety
of dishes which are made of meat, chicken, fish
or vegetables. The method of cooking also varies, from
roasting to grilling, frying and braising. *Khoraks* always have
very little or no sauce at all, in contrast to *khoresh*, which
has plenty of sauce. They are usually eaten with bread. The
regional diversity of *khoraks* is best exemplified in stuffed
fish dishes. The main types of stuffing used in the north
are walnut, dates and mint in pomegranate sauce (p. 99). In
the south fish is usually stuffed with herbs like coriander/
cilantro, garlic and chilli (p. 111).

Roast duck with *fesenjan*
sauce, served here with
Morassa polo

Roast chicken stuffed with mixed nuts, orange and lemon juliennes

Morghe-e tanoori ba limo va portoghal

SERVES 4
PREPARATION about 20
   minutes
COOKING about 1½ hours

INGREDIENTS

1 chicken (weighing 1.8–2 kg/
   4–4½ lb)
1 medium onion
2 celery sticks
2 medium oranges
2 large lemons
30 g/1 oz flaked almonds
30 g/1 oz pistachio slivers
30 g/1 oz crushed walnuts
2 teaspoons dried lime powder
1 teaspoon ground cinnamon
2 tablespoons liquid saffron
   (*see* INGREDIENTS)
30 g/1 oz butter
2 tablespoons vegetable oil
salt and pepper

This recipe is a variation on a traditional one from the Azerbaijan province of north-west Iran.

Different combinations of citrus and dried fruits with nuts mixed with herbs, sweet spices and saffron are used to stuff poultry. The aroma gets diffused into the meat and the tangy flavoursome stuffing counterbalances the plain meat of the chicken.

PREPARATION

Heat the oven to 220°C/425°F/gas mark 7.

Trim off any excess fat inside and outside the chicken; wash and dry it, and then sprinkle with salt and pepper.

Using a small sharp knife or a peeler, peel the oranges and lemons, trimming away as much pith as possible. Cut the pieces of peel into uniform juliennes. To extract the bitterness of the orange and lemon peel, place them in a small saucepan of water and bring to the boil. Remove from the heat and drain in a sieve. Taste the peel and repeat the blanching if it is still bitter. Drain the peel and set to one side. Juice the oranges and the lemon.

Peel and slice the onion. Chop the celery sticks into pieces no bigger than 1 cm/½ inch square.

COOKING

Heat the oil and half of the butter in a heavy-based frying pan. Fry the onions to golden, add the chopped celery, fry for a couple of minutes and then add the lemon and orange juliennes, walnuts, almond and pistachio slivers, cinnamon and dried lime powder. Stir-fry for a minute, remove and set to one side to cool down completely.

Place the chicken breast-up on a roasting tin and stuff the cavity with the stuffing mix. Mix the saffron with lemon and orange juice and pour all over the chicken; dot with the rest of the butter. Roast for 20 minutes in the middle of the oven. Then turn the chicken over, breast-down, reduce the oven to 200°C/400°F/gas mark 6 and roast for a further 30 minutes. Finally turn the chicken breast-up again, and continue roasting for another 30 minutes.

Before serving, pour the juices from the pan over the chicken and let it rest for 10 minutes.

Serve with saffron jewelled rice or plain rice (p. 134). A mixed salad with vinegar dressing is a nice accompaniment.

Roast duck with pomegranate and walnut sauce

Khorak-e morghabi

SERVES 4
PREPARATION about 15
minutes
COOKING about 2½ hours

INGREDIENTS

1 duck (weighing 2–2.2
kg/4½–5 lb)
200 ml/7 fl oz honey
1 medium onion
250 g/9 oz shelled walnuts
3 tablespoons vegetable oil
500 ml/1 pint chicken stock
350 ml/12 fl oz pomegranate
syrup
3 tablespoons sugar
salt and pepper

This dish is a variation on the traditional duck *fesenjan*, which is a thick *khoresh*. I prefer to roast the whole duck separately because I can discard the fat that is generated during cooking. The pomegranate and walnut sauce is rich, so it is preferable not to cook the duck in it as the dish would be too oily.

New Persian Cooking contains a recipe for chicken with walnut and pomegranate (chicken *fesenjan*).

PREPARATION

Heat the oven to 220°C/425°F/gas mark 7.

Wash the duck and thoroughly dry it. Cut off the end bits of the wing and remove the excess fat from the cavity. Place the duck, breast-up, on a roasting rack in a tin and with a sharp knife make a very shallow slit diagonally through the breast skin on both sides and pierce the skin of the legs. This helps the fat to drain better.

Sprinkle with salt and pepper and let it stand in room temperature for 2 hours before cooking.

Peel and finely chop the onion.

Grind the walnuts in a food processor.

COOKING

Pour the honey all over the duck and place it in the middle of the oven, breast-up; roast for 30 minutes. Remove from the oven and turn the duck over, breast-down, and discard the fat that has collected in the tin. Return to the oven and roast for a further 30 minutes. Repeat the procedure: remove from the oven, turn the duck on its back, discard the fat and

return to the oven; reduce the temperature to 180°C/350°F/ gas mark 4 and roast for 1½ hours. To check whether the duck is ready or not, poke a skewer into the thickest park of the leg: the juices should run clear.

Whilst the duck is cooking, prepare the sauce. In a heavy-based saucepan heat the oil and fry the onion to golden, add the ground walnuts, stir, and fry for a couple of minutes; add the chicken stock, the pomegranate syrup and the sugar, stir well, reduce the heat and simmer for 40–45 minutes. The sauce should be thick and practically black. Check the seasoning; add more sugar if you prefer it sweeter or add more pomegranate syrup for a sharper taste.

Take the duck out of the oven 15 minutes before serving to allow it to rest. Cut the legs from the hip joint and the breast into halves across the wishbone.

Arrange the pieces in a shallow serving dish, garnish with fresh mint or parsley. Serve the sauce in a bowl.

Duck with pomegranate and walnut sauce goes well with saffron rice. A green salad would be a refreshing addition.

fesenjan sauce

Roast partridge with herb and walnut stuffing

Kabk-e tanoori

Partridge and, to a lesser extent, pheasant are prevalent game birds all over the country. Partridge *kabab* (grilled on charcoal) with saffron and lemon juice is the most popular recipe.

I prefer to roast the partridge with a herb stuffing because the meat retains its moisture better and the stuffing infuses the much-needed aroma to the dish. Game birds, being less fatty than others, tend to dry out quickly when grilled.

PREPARATION

Heat the oven to 200°C/400°F/gas mark 6.

Wash and dry the partridges.

Wash the herbs, remove the tough stalks, and dry. With a wide-bladed knife chop the herbs finely. Chop one of the onions finely and slice the other. Chop the garlic finely.

COOKING

Heat 2 tablespoons of oil and a tablespoon of butter in a frying pan and fry the chopped onions until translucent, then add the chopped garlic and fry for a minute.

Add the chopped herbs, turmeric, salt and pepper and fry for 3–4 minutes. Remove from the heat and allow to cool down. Mix the ground walnuts with 1 tablespoon of butter and fold into the herb mixture.

Stuff each partridge with the herb and walnut mix; sprinkle the birds with salt and pepper.

In a large frying pan melt the rest of the butter with the rest of the oil and seal the partridges on all sides until golden.

SERVES 4
PREPARATION about 20 minutes
COOKING about 1 hour

INGREDIENTS

4 partridges
200 ml/7 fl oz chicken stock
2 medium onions
3 large cloves of garlic
50 g/2 oz parsley
50 g/2 oz coriander/cilantro
150 g/5 oz ground walnuts
50 g/2 oz butter
4 tablespoons vegetable oil
3 tablespoons lemon juice or wine vinegar
½ teaspoon turmeric
2 dessertspoons sugar
salt and pepper to taste

Arrange the sliced onion at the bottom of a roasting dish and place the birds, breast-down, over the onion slices. Add the stock, lemon juice or vinegar and sugar, check the seasoning and cook in the oven for 20 minutes. Turn the birds over, so they are breast-up now, return to the oven and cook for a further 20 minutes. Make sure not to overcook the partridges as they can easily dry out.

Remove the partridges to a serving plate, keep warm. Blend the juices in a blender and pour over the birds.

Serve with warm bread, sweet chutney (mango or lime) and a side dish of carrot and sultana salad.

Sour chicken with herbs

Morgh-e torsh

This recipe comes from the province of Gilan, on the Caspian sea, in the north of Iran. The area is lush and rich in a wide variety of herbs that are used in different combinations with meat, poultry and fish. The majority of dishes are sweet-and-sour with a dominant lemon and sour (Seville) orange taste.

I enjoyed this dish as a child in my paternal grandfather's house in the north of the country. Memories are revived when I cook it now, in England, so many years later. I believe that the memory of events is often food-related; as though food helps us put together bits of the past and give it cohesion.

I have added tarragon, which goes well with chicken, to the recipe.

PREPARATION

Skin the chicken pieces. Dry them on paper kitchen towel. Rub the chicken pieces with the zest and the juice of the lemon.

Peel and finely chop the garlic cloves. Peel and roughly chop the onion.

Wash the herbs, remove the tough stalks, and dry them thoroughly in a salad crisper. With a sharp wide-bladed knife chop them finely.

Pour boiling water over the split peas and soak for a couple of hours.

SERVES 4
PREPARATION about 20 minutes plus soaking
COOKING about 1 hour

INGREDIENTS

8 chicken pieces (preferably skinless thighs) on the bone
300 g/11 oz parsley
100 g/3½ oz coriander/cilantro
50 g/2 oz tarragon
50 g/2 oz split peas
1 teaspoon turmeric
200 ml/7 fl oz chicken stock
3 tablespoons lemon juice and half a lemon
1 medium onion
5 6 cloves of garlic
salt and pepper to taste
30 g/1 oz butter
2 tablespoons vegetable oil

COOKING

In a medium-sized saucepan melt half of the butter and the oil. Fry the chicken pieces until golden; take them out with a slotted spoon and put to one side. Add the rest of the oil and the butter to the saucepan, fry the onion until golden, add the garlic, fry for one minute, then add the herbs and the turmeric, continue frying for 4–5 minutes. Add the chicken pieces and the split peas (after draining) and the lemon juice and then the stock.

Cover, reduce the heat and simmer for about 45–50 minutes until the chicken is cooked. The sauce should be quite thick.

Serve with warm flatbread or plain rice and a side dish of yogurt with celery or yogurt with cucumber.

Stuffed shoulder of lamb with dried fruits, orange and almond in pomegranate syrup

Sardast-e barreh topour

Dried fruits mixed with nuts and orange or lemon are a popular stuffing mix in the north of Iran. The stuffing is deliciously aromatic, diffusing full flavour into the meat, giving it a fresh taste.

This recipe is a variation on the traditional one. I like to use a shoulder of lamb with the bone left in as it helps the meat to remains moist throughout the long cooking period. I don't use rice in the stuffing mix, so the stuffing is lighter and juicier.

PREPARATION

Heat the oven to 180°C/350°F/gas mark 4.

Wash the lamb and trim off any extra fat. With a sharp knife make a cut in the middle as deep as possible, creating a pocket for the stuffing. Sprinkle with salt and pepper.

Peel and roughly chop the onion. Chop the apricots; thinly slice one of the oranges and juice the other.

Juice the lemon and soak the sultanas in 1 tablespoon of the juice mixed with 1 teaspoon of liquid saffron.

COOKING

In a frying pan, heat the oil and fry the onion to golden and then add the chopped apricots and orange slices. Drain the sultanas and add to the pan, followed by the almonds. Stir-fry for a couple of minutes; add the turmeric, *advieh* and pomegranate syrup. Stir to mix well and remove from the heat. Allow to cool down. When cool, stuff the shoulder of lamb with the mix, filling the pocket.

SERVES 4
PREPARATION about 15 minutes
COOKING about 3½ hours

INGREDIENTS

1 medium-sized shoulder of lamb (with the bone in)
1 medium onion
2 large oranges
1 lemon
100 g/3½ oz dried apricot
100 g/3½ oz sultana
50 g/2 oz crushed almonds (almond flakes crushed in a pestle and mortar)
150 ml/5 fl oz pomegranate syrup
1 teaspoon turmeric
1 teaspoon *advieh* for meat (see INGREDIENTS)
4 tablespoons liquid saffron (*see* INGREDIENTS)
4 tablespoons vegetable oil
50 g/2 oz butter
salt and pepper

Either place the stuffed shoulder in an oven-proof casserole dish with a lid, or make a parcel from a double layer of aluminium foil so that the meat is completely sealed in. Melt the butter, add 2 teaspoons of liquid saffron and the orange juice and pour over the lamb. Cover with a lid or fold over the foil. Roast in the middle of the oven for approximately 3 hours (allow approximately 30 minutes per 450 g/1 lb). The meat should be thoroughly cooked and soft, separating from the bone easily with a fork.

Remove the lid or open the foil, baste the meat with juice and roast open for a further 20–30 minutes until golden brown.

Serve with herbs or dill and broad bean rice (see the recipes in *New Persian Cooking*). A dish of yogurt and a plate of herbs (*sabzi khordan*) or a mixed salad are great accompaniments to this dish.

Sardast-e barreh topour

Stuffed trout with walnuts, dates and mint in pomegranate syrup

Mahi-e topour

In the regions by the Caspian Sea in the north of Iran and in those around the Persian Gulf in the south, fish dishes are prevalent. There are numerous varieties of fish, and those from the Caspian are distinctly different to those living in the Persian Gulf. As might be expected, the recipes also differ in many respects. What is common is the preference for stuffing the fish and baking it in a clay oven. Not many people in the West have a clay oven; however, good results can be had by grilling the fish. (If you do happen to have a pizza oven, I urge you to roast fish in it.)

The stuffing mix in the north is usually sweet-and-sour, using dried fruits, nuts and herbs with pomegranate syrup or plenty of lemon juice and saffron; whilst in the south the mix is made with plenty of garlic and chillies, turmeric and other spices in tamarind juice.

The stuffing mix of this recipe is suitable for a wide variety of fish. You can use sea bass, sea bream, snapper, even salmon. I have chosen trout because it is more oily (easier to grill), widely available and is not expensive.

This dish is easy to prepare but do allow enough time for the stuffing to be made and cool down before filling the fish.

SERVES 4
PREPARATION about 15 minutes
COOKING about 30 minutes

INGREDIENTS

4 small trout
1 medium onion
4 cloves of garlic
50 g/2 oz crushed walnuts
50 g/2 oz chopped dates
50 g/2 oz sultanas or raisins
30 g/1 oz chopped fresh or frozen mint
juice and zest of 1 lemon
100 ml/3½ fl oz pomegranate syrup
30 g/1 oz butter
2 tablespoons vegetable oil
salt and pepper

PREPARATION

Wash the fish thoroughly and dry. Wash the mint, dry and chop coarsely. (In the summer I prepare mint in this way and then freeze it in portions of 25–30 g/1 oz.) Crush the walnuts in a pestle and mortar until the pieces are approximately 50 mm; do not pulverise them. Peel and finely chop the onion and the garlic. Chop the dates into small pieces.

COOKING

Rub the trout with salt and pepper and half of the lemon, scatter the zest inside and out and marinate them in the juice for about 30 minutes before cooking.

Heat the oil and 1 tablespoon of the butter in a medium-sized frying pan and fry the onion to golden brown. Add the garlic, stir and fry for 1 minute. Add the sultanas (or raisins), dates and mint and fry for a couple of minutes. Add the walnuts and the pomegranate syrup, stir, remove from the heat and mix well. Set to one side to cool down. Then stuff each trout with a tablespoon of the mixture. Arrange the fish on a well-oiled baking tray and dot them with butter.

Grill the trout on maximum heat in the middle position for 10 minutes each side. Take care when turning them over.

In Iran fish is almost always served with either herb or plain rice. I prefer this dish with plain rice and a green salad with celery and apple in a lemon juice dressing.

Stuffed poussin with prunes and herbs in pomegranate sauce

Morgh-e topour

In the north of Iran on the Caspian Sea, the typical way of stuffing chicken, and even fish, is to use aromatic herbs combined with fruits in a sweet-and-sour sauce. In this recipe I have substituted tarragon for one of the herbs traditionally used, which is not readily available. My preference is to use poussins, but a small chicken may be preferred.

PREPARATION

Wash the poussins and trim off the extra skin and fat. Dry thoroughly. Peel and chop the garlic cloves. Peel and chop the onion.

Soak the prunes in hot water.

Clean the herbs, separate the green and fresh leaves and tender stalks and discard the rest. Wash the herbs in plenty of water and dry them. Chop them finely using a sharp wide-bladed knife.

COOKING

In a large frying pan heat 2 tablespoons of oil and fry the onion until golden; add the chopped garlic and fry for 1 minute. Drain the prunes and add to the pan, stir well and then add the chopped herbs and 1 teaspoon of turmeric. Fry for about 5 minutes, stirring frequently to mix all the ingredients thoroughly. Lower the heat and add 100 ml/3½ fl oz of pomegranate syrup, mix well. Remove from the heat and allow to cool down.

Rub the poussins with the skin and the zest of the lemon, sprinkle some salt and pepper all over. Stuff the poussins with half of the herb and prune mixture and close the cavity loosely.

SERVES 4
PREPARATION about 20 minutes
COOKING about 50 minutes for poussin; 1¼ hours for chicken

INGREDIENTS

2 poussins (or a small chicken of about 1.5 kg/3½ lb)
8 cloves of garlic
1 teaspoon turmeric
1 large onion
100 g/3½ oz parsley
100 g/3½ oz chives
50 g/2 oz coriander/cilantro
30 g/1 oz tarragon
2 dessertspoons dried fenugreek
200 g/7 oz prunes (or *aaloo Bokhara* yellow prunes)
250 ml/9 fl oz pomegranate syrup
2 dessertspoons sugar
3 tablespoons vegetable oil
zest and juice of 1 lemon
salt and pepper

In a saucepan big enough to accommodate the poussins heat the rest of the oil and carefully fry the poussins until golden all over (around 10 minutes). Add to the pan the rest of the herb and prune mix, the remaining pomegranate juice, the sugar and a cup of boiling water. Lower the heat and simmer for 40–50 minutes until the poussins are cooked (if you are using a chicken, it will need about 1¼ hours). The sauce should be thick and dark green (nearly black) in colour.

Serve in a shallow dish. Take the poussins carefully out of the pan and arrange the herb and prune sauce around them.

This dish goes well with plain rice and a side dish of yogurt.

Braised lamb with beetroot, sultana, celery and potato

Taaskabab-e choghondar

The nearest equivalent to *taaskabab i*s braising or pot-roasting.

There is a wide variety of *taaskabab*, but the basis of them all is lamb, onion and various vegetables arranged in layers in a pot and cooked very slowly on a low heat over 3 hours. The meat is usually shoulder of lamb cut into chunks; the vegetables can be anything from carrots, beetroot and celery to tomatoes and courgettes. It can also include fruits like quince and dried fruits such as apricots and raisins.

In this *taaskabab* beetroot, lemon and sultanas are mixed with fresh mint and celery to create a fresh aromatic mix.

PREPARATION

Heat the oven to 180°C/350°F/gas mark 4.

Wash the lamb and trim off the excess fat, cut the meat into pieces of 2 cm/¾ inch thickness by 5–6 cm/2–2½ inches in length, sprinkle with salt and pepper.

Peel and slice the onion, beetroot and potatoes into 1 cm/½ inch-thick pieces. Wash and finely chop the celery. Wash and slice the lemon thinly, remove the pith. Wash the mint leaves. Soak the sultanas in a cup of warm water for 10–15 minutes.

COOKING

You need a deep and thick-based casserole dish or earthenware pot. Arrange a layer of sliced onions at the bottom, followed by a layer of meat and then beetroot,

SERVES 4
PREPARATION about 15 minutes
COOKING about 3 hours

INGREDIENTS

500 g/1 lb 2 oz boneless shoulder of lamb
1 large onion
250 g/9 oz sweet beetroot
250 g/9 oz potato (any type)
3–4 celery sticks
20 g/¾ oz fresh mint leaves
100 g/3½ oz sultanas
1 lemon (preferably unwaxed)
2 tablespoons lemon juice
1 teaspoon ground cinnamon
2 tablespoons liquid saffron (*see* INGREDIENTS)
20 g/¾ oz butter

potato, celery, sultanas and mint. Repeat if you have ingredients left. Arrange the lemon slices with more mint leaves on the top. Melt the butter in a small saucepan, remove from the heat and add the lemon juice and liquid saffron, stir in the cinnamon; pour over the ingredients in the pot. Close the pot tightly and roast for approximately 3 hours.

Remove from the oven, allow to stand for 10 minutes and then take to the table in the same pot.

Taaskabab is eaten with warm flatbread, fresh herbs (*sabzi khordan*) and yogurt.

NOTE It is important to choose young small beetroots, as the dish can otherwise become bitter and tart.

Taaskabab-e choghondar

Spicy chicken in coconut sauce

Morgh ba sheer-e narghill

On the way from Shiraz, the city of my birth, to my grand-father's house on the Persian Gulf there was a café famous for its chicken dish; we always stopped there for lunch. I still remember the delicious aroma of the succulent poussins.

This recipe is my version of the chicken dish that I had as a child in that roadside café. I have added coconut milk, which blends well with the spices and ties the dish together.

PREPARATION

Skin the chicken pieces or poussins and wash them. Dry them on paper kitchen towel. Rub the chicken pieces or poussin with the zest and the juice of the half lemon.

Peel and finely chop the garlic. Peel and roughly chop the onion.

In a large bowl combine the coriander, ginger, cinnamon, chilli powder, half of the saffron liquid, chopped garlic and onion and half of the peanut oil. Add the poussins or chicken pieces to the bowl, rubbing the paste all over the outside and inside of the meat. Marinate for at least 6 hours or overnight.

COOKING

In a large-size saucepan heat the rest of the oil. Fry the poussins or chicken pieces with the marinade mixture until lightly golden. Add the other half of the liquid saffron, lemon juice and stock. Fold in the coconut milk.

Cover, reduce the heat and simmer for about half an hour until the chicken is tender. The sauce should be quite thick at this stage. Add the tomato purée and cook for another 5 to 10 minutes.

SERVES 4
PREPARATION about 15 minutes plus marinating
COOKING about 45–50 minutes

INGREDIENTS

2 poussins or 6 small chicken pieces (2 skinless breasts, 4 skinless thighs)
2 teaspoons ground coriander/cilantro seeds
1½ teaspoons fresh ginger (grated or very finely chopped)
1 teaspoon ground cinnamon
1 teaspoon chilli powder (more if you like a spicier taste)
5–6 cloves of garlic
1 large onion
150 ml/5 fl oz chicken stock
4 tablespoons liquid saffron (*see* INGREDIENTS)
3 tablespoons lemon juice and the zest of 1 lime and 1 lemon
1 teaspoon tomato purée
200 ml/7 fl oz coconut milk
3 tablespoons peanut or vegetable oil
salt and pepper to taste

Serve on a flat dish and cover the chicken with the sauce.

This dish goes well with plain rice and side dishes of chilli pickles, fresh herbs and/or shallot yogurt. It is equally nice with warm flatbread or garlic bread.

VARIATION

You can replace coconut milk with yogurt. Cook the chicken in the stock, reduce, remove from the heat to cool down slightly. Add 2 tablespoons of Greek-style yogurt, stir and serve.

Spicy chicken thighs with potato and chillies

Morgh ba seebzamini va advieh

This is a wonderfully spicy dish from Bushehr on the Persian Gulf. The combination of aromatic spices and chicken with potato sticks work well. It is easy to prepare and cook.

PREPARATION

Wash the thigh fillets, trim off any excess fat. Dry them on paper kitchen towel. Rub them with the lemon skin.

Peel and finely chop the garlic and chillies. Peel and roughly chop the onion.

In a pestle and mortar crush the chillies and garlic; add coriander, ginger, cinnamon and cumin and mix well.

Peel the potatoes and cut them lengthways into ½ cm/¼ inch-thick sticks, keep in cool water.

COOKING

In a large saucepan heat half of the oil and butter. Fry the chicken pieces until lightly golden. Take them out with a slotted spoon and keep warm. In the same pan heat the rest of the oil and butter and fry the onion until golden Now add the turmeric, spice, garlic and chilli mix and stir-fry for a couple of minutes. Return the chicken pieces to the pan, add the tomato purée and stir well to mix all the ingredients. Add the stock, bring to the boil.

Cover, reduce the heat and simmer for about 40 minutes until the chicken is tender. The sauce should be quite thick at this stage. If it is not, reduce the sauce further. Add the lemon juice and salt and pepper to taste.

SERVES 4
PREPARATION about 15 minutes
COOKING about 1 hour

INGREDIENTS

8 skinless chicken thigh fillets
1 medium onion
8 cloves of garlic
500 g/1 lb 2 oz salad or small new potatoes
1 teaspoon turmeric
1 or 2 hot chillies
1 teaspoon grated fresh ginger
1 tablespoon coriander seeds
1 teaspoon ground cinnamon
1 teaspoon ground cumin
1 tablespoon tomato purée
300 ml/10 fl oz chicken stock
juice of 1 large lemon
30 g/1 oz butter
4 tablespoons vegetable oil and enough for frying the potato
salt and pepper to taste

Now in a frying pan heat enough oil to fry the potatoes. Drain and dry the potato sticks and add to the oil, fry until golden.

Serve the chicken fillets on a flat dish and place the fried potatoes on top.

This dish is ideal with warm pitta bread and a green salad or a side plate of fresh herbs (*sabzi khordan*).

Roast poussins with cherry tomatoes, red and yellow peppers

Joojeh tanoori ba gojehfaranghi

Layers of taste and aroma are the feature of this dish, where roasted tomatoes and peppers set off the poussins on their bed of onion. I prefer poussins for roasting; alternatively a small free-range chicken can be used.

This is an easy dish to prepare and cook, and is both tasty and aesthetically pleasing.

PREPARATION

Heat the oven to 200°C/400°F/gas mark 6.

Wash the poussins and trim off any extra skin and fat. Dry thoroughly. Peel and crush the garlic.

In a bowl, mix the crushed garlic, 4 tablespoons of olive oil, the lemon zest and juice and 2 tablespoons of liquid saffron. Rub the poussins with salt and pepper and the skin of the squeezed lemon. Slide your hands between the skin and the breast to separate them, spread the mixture of crushed garlic, lemon and olive oil between the breast and the skin, and cover the chickens with the remainder of the mix.

Wash the capsicums, remove the stalk, cut in two lengthways, and cut each half into two pieces.

Peel and cut the onion into 4–5 wedges.

COOKING

Put the onion wedges in a shallow oven tray and place the poussins on top. Dot with butter and arrange the pepper/capsicum pieces and cherry tomatoes around the poussins; sprinkle olive oil on the tomatoes and the peppers. Bake for 45–50 minutes. (A chicken will take longer, around 1¼ hours.) Turn the birds once halfway through.

SERVES 4
PREPARATION about 10 minutes
COOKING about 45 minutes for a poussin; 1¼ hours for a chicken

INGREDIENTS

2 poussins (or 1 chicken weighing 1.5–1.8 kg/3–4 lb)
5 large cloves of garlic
1 medium onion
1 red pepper/capsicum
1 yellow pepper/capsicum
10–12 cherry tomatoes
4 tablespoons extra virgin olive oil
juice and zest of 1 lemon
2 tablespoons liquid saffron (*see* INGREDIENTS)
30 g/1 oz butter

Before serving, remove from the oven and allow to stand
for 10 minutes. Arrange in a serving dish and pour any
remaining juice over the poussins.

Serve with jacket potatoes or bread and a green salad.

Joojeh tanoori ba gojehfaranghi

Roast fish stuffed with roast garlic, chillies and tamarind juice

Mahi topour ba seer va felefel

The nearest readily available Western equivalent to the white fish that are caught in the Persian Gulf (such as *shoorideh*) is sea bass. However, other types of fish, such as sea bream and snapper, will do just as well, and even a river fish like trout may be used.

Traditionally the stuffing is made with plenty of garlic and very hot chillies. I use roasted garlic as it is more aromatic and makes a smoother stuffing mix.

PREPARATION

Wash and dry the fish. Rub them with salt, pepper and the lime zest inside and out; marinate them in the zest and the juice of the lime.

Peel the onion and slice. Prepare the tamarind juice. Chop the chillies.

To prepare the garlic, heat the oven to 200°C/400°F/gas mark 6. Peel away the outer layers of the whole garlic bulbs. With a sharp knife cut ½ cm/¼ inch off the tops of the bulbs, exposing the cloves. Drizzle a few drops of olive oil on top of each garlic bulb, wrap the garlic loosely in foil and bake in a small ovenproof dish for 30 minutes. Allow to cool, squeeze the flesh out of each clove.

COOKING

Heat the oil in a small frying pan and fry the sliced onion until golden. Add the chillies and turmeric and fry for 1 minute. Fold in the roasted garlic and strained tamarind juice, stir well and set to one side to cool.

SERVES 4
PREPARATION about 30 minutes
COOKING about 15–20 minutes

INGREDIENTS

2 medium-sized whole sea bass
1 small onion
2 large bulbs of garlic
2 or 3 hot green chillies (more if you like a spicier taste)
2 teaspoons turmeric
20 g/¾ oz tamarind paste dissolved in 100 ml/3½ fl oz boiling water
2 tablespoons vegetable oil
1 tablespoon butter
juice and zest of 1 lime (preferably unwaxed)
salt and pepper

Stuff each fish with the mix, arrange the fish on a well-oiled baking tray (preferably covered with aluminium foil), dot with butter. Grill on maximum heat for about 15 minutes, turning the fish over, with care, halfway through.

Place in a flat dish, garnished with coriander/cilantro or parsley (optional); serve with plain rice and a green salad like rocket.

Fried prawns with potato sticks and onion

Dupiazeh maygoo

SERVES 4

PREPARATION about 10 minutes

COOKING about 10–15 minutes

INGREDIENTS

500 g/1 lb 2 oz peeled large prawns/shrimps
1 large onion
4 cloves of garlic
1 teaspoon grated fresh ginger
1 teaspoon chilli flakes
4 tablespoons vegetable oil
1 teaspoon turmeric
1 teaspoon powdered dried lime (see INGREDIENTS)
100 g/3½ oz sultanas (optional)
salt and pepper to taste

FOR THE POTATO STICKS

3 medium potatoes (King Edward or baking potatoes)
Enough vegetable oil to fry the potato sticks

In the southern city of Bushehr, where my maternal grandfather came from, prawns used to be plentiful and cheap, and therefore almost a staple food of the region. Prawn is the main ingredient in many delicious dishes from the south like *maygoo polo* (prawn rice) and *ghalyeh maygoo* (prawn casserole with coriander in tamarind juice) (see the recipes in *New Persian Cooking*).

Dupiazeh – frying with plenty of onion – is a popular way of cooking vegetable and fish dishes in the south of the country. This dish of prawns fried with onions with the addition of spices and sultanas is a delicious dish typical of Bushehr. It is a well-balanced meal with both protein and carbohydrate.

It is traditionally made with shrimps, but I prefer to make it with larger prawns for a main course.

PREPARATION

Peel the onion and finely slice it.

Crush the garlic cloves.

Peel the potatoes and cut them into sticks of about ½ cm/¼ inch thickness.

COOKING

In a large frying pan heat the oil and fry the onions until golden. Take out with a slotted spoon and set to one side. In the same pan, fry the garlic and the ginger for 1 minute, add the prawns, turmeric, dried lime and the sultanas (if using), stir fry for 4–5 minutes. Reduce the heat and return the fried onions, stir to mix with the rest of the ingredients. Remove from the heat and keep warm.

In a separate pan bring to a medium heat enough vegetable oil to cover the potatoes. Fry the potato sticks in batches, letting each batch drain on paper kitchen towel. Serve the prawn mix in a shallow dish, sprinkle the chilli flakes over; place the fried potatoes on top.

This dish goes well with garlic bread, a side dish of green salad and a hot chutney (chilli and coriander, hot mango chutney).

KABAB

THE WORD *kabab* in Persian means to grill skewers of meat over red-hot charcoal.

Skewers of lamb fillet (*kabab-e barg*) together with minced meat kabab (*kaba-e kubideh*), eaten with plain rice (*chelo*), comprise the national dish *chelo-kabab*. If you have been to a Persian restaurant, it is more than likely that you have eaten *chelo kabab*. Even Persians, who prefer to cook more complex dishes at home, will go to a restaurant for *chelo kebab*, and in Iran they used to refer to restaurants as *chelo kababi* – the place for *chelo kabab*.

A great deal of ritual is involved in preparing and eating *chelo kabab*: The *chelo* rice has to be perfectly cooked and fluffy, decorated with liquid saffron. The meat has to come from the best cuts, usually tenderloin of lamb delicately filleted and marinated in a mix of grated onion, saffron and lemon juice. Kabab has to be cooked through but must remain moist; the meat needs to have some fat content so that during grilling over the very hot charcoal it retains its moisture.

The accompanying dishes are an essential part of eating *chelo kabab*; without them the dish would be just a skewer of meat with rice. Grilled tomatoes are a must. You also need to have a yogurt side dish, either with dried shallots or cucumber, a plate of fresh herbs (*sabzi khordan*) to include tarragon, basil, radishes and spring onions (or red onion).

Traditionally the yolk of an egg is placed on each diner's plate in the middle of the rice (you can omit the raw egg if you wish), then a knob of butter, and a generous sprinkling of *sumac* (an essential addition; see INGREDIENTS); then everything is mixed. You eat a piece of grilled tomato and a piece of kabab with a spoonful of your rice mixture and experience Persian cuisine at its simplest yet most delicious.

Kababs are also eaten wrapped in freshly baked flatbread with barbecued tomatoes and fresh herbs.

Joojeh kabab

Chunky lamb fillet kabab

Kabab-e kenjeh

SERVES 4
PREPARATION AND
COOKING about 20 minutes
plus marinating

INGREDIENTS
500 g/1 lb 2 oz lamb fillet
    (tenderloin)
1 medium onion
2 tablespoons lemon juice
4 tablespoons liquid saffron
    (*see* INGREDIENTS)
50 g/2 oz butter

This is a variation of lamb fillet kabab, in Persian *barg kabab* (see the recipe for *chelo kabab barg* in *New Persian Cooking*). There is a wide range of *kabab-e kenjeh* using different marinades and various cuts of meat.

I prefer to make this with lamb tenderloin in a saffron and lemon juice marinade. This kabab should ideally be cooked over red-hot charcoal, but the skewers can be grilled if you do not have a barbecue.

PREPARATION AND COOKING

Peel the onion and grate it. Wash the meat and cut into 3–4 cm/1½ inch cubes. In a large bowl, mix the grated onion, the lemon juice, 2 tablespoons of liquid saffron and salt and pepper. Place the lamb cubes in the bowl, mix well to coat all the cubes, marinate for at least 2 hours, more if possible.

Thread the meat onto thin metal skewers. Ensure the charcoal barbecue is very hot; if using a grill, set it to maximum. Melt the butter and mix with the remaining saffron liquid; baste the meat during barbecuing or grilling. The skewers should be placed very near the charcoal or close to the grill. Turn frequently and cook until the edges of the meat cubes turn brown (approximately 10 minutes). The meat should be cooked through but remain moist.

Kabab-e kenjeh is often served in the middle of warm flatbread with grilled tomatoes and a sprinkling of *sumac*. It is equally delicious with rice. A side dish of yogurt and cucumber or yogurt and wild shallots (*maast va moosir*, p. 200), and of course fresh herbs and spring onions, go very well with it.

Chicken kabab

Joojeh kabab

Chicken kabab, or rather poussin (*joojeh*) kabab, is a very popular favourite in Iran. There used to be specialist restaurants that served only chicken kebab, and these were called *joojeh kababi*. They used charcoal barbecues to grill the poussins. They had a long built-in trough stretching along one wall filled with red-hot coals where the birds, marinated overnight, were grilled as orders came in.

Most of these restaurants had wonderful gardens where they arranged the tables around the fountains on summer evenings. I still remember the smell of the barbecue mixed with the scent of freshly watered lawn, a refreshing breeze passing over the hedges and through the leaves of the old maple trees.

PREPARATION

Ask your butcher to spatchcock the poussins for you. Alternatively do it yourself: with a sharp knife, cut along either side of the back; then flatten the chicken on a chopping board into a butterfly shape.

Wash and dry the poussins on paper kitchen towel.

With a sharp knife make incisions across the skin on the thigh flesh and across the flattened chickens through the breast fillets. This is done to let the marinade penetrate the flesh where it is thickest. It also allows the heat to cook the chicken evenly.

To make the marinade, mix the ingredients in a shallow dish big enough to take the birds side by side. Brush the chicken with the marinade to cover them inside and out. Cover the dish with clingfilm and set to one side for at least

SERVES 4
PREPARATION about 20–25 minutes
COOKING 30–35 minutes

INGREDIENTS

2 poussins

FOR THE MARINADE

2 cloves of garlic, peeled and crushed
juice of 1 large lemon
2 tablespoons liquid saffron (*see* INGREDIENTS)
4 tablespoons olive oil
salt and pepper to taste

a couple of hours. Turn the birds every half an hour in the marinade. Better still, leave them in the marinade overnight in the fridge.

COOKING

To grill the chickens, you need a very hot barbeque or grill. If it is big enough to allow the two birds to be grilled at the same time, so much the better. Grill each side for approximately 10–15 minutes and baste occasionally with olive oil. Check to make sure that they are cooked through to the bone; if not, allow a further 5 minutes on each side.

You can use a grill instead of the barbeque to cook the birds. Have the grill on its highest setting. Put the chicken on a rack in the middle of the grill with an oven tray underneath. Cook for 10–15 minutes on each side and baste with olive oil as above.

Serve hot off the grill with plain rice or warm flatbread and side dishes of tomato salad, yogurt and cucumber and a hot pickle.

TIP Use two flat skewers to pierce through the thigh and the breast on either side to facilitate moving the birds on the grill or to turn them over.

KOOKOO

K OOKOO is a flavoursome combination of herbs and vegetables, with egg. *Kookoo* is loosely translated as simply 'omelette' but it is in fact quite different, being more like Spanish *tortilla* or an Italian *frittata*. That is, the egg is not dominant as in the classic Western dish, but is used rather as a base for the main ingredients.

Numerous versions of *kookoo* are cooked across the country. Many different permutations of herbs and vegetables are used, including beans, potatoes and aubergine. *Kookoo sabzi* (herb omelette – see the recipe in *New Persian Cooking*) is the most famous and is more popular than the others.

Kookoo is a delicious vegetarian meal that can be served hot as a main course or cold as a side dish or as a snack. It is eaten with hot bread and must always be served with some kind of pickle (such as garlic or mango or mixed pickle) and a yogurt dish to bring out the flavours.

Narghesi-e esfenaj

Aubergine omelette

Kookoo-ye badenjan

SERVES 4
PREPARATION about 20–30
  minutes
COOKING about 1 hour

INGREDIENTS

6 eggs
3 medium aubergines
2 medium onions
1 dessertspoon plain flour
1 teaspoon bicarbonate of soda
2 tablespoons liquid saffron
  (*see* INGREDIENTS)
30 g/1 oz butter
2 tablespoons vegetable oil
oil for frying
salt and pepper

Aubergine, smoked or fried, mixed with egg is a great favourite all over Iran. The aubergine *kookoo* is a delicious vegetarian meal; it is always eaten as a light main course with bread.

You can grill (preferably chargrill over charcoal) or fry the aubergine. I fry the aubergines in a little oil and put them on paper kitchen towel to remove as much of the oil as possible before combining with the other ingredients; the consistency of the *kookoo* tends to be smoother.

PREPARATION

Peel the aubergines with a potato peeler and slice them lengthways into 3 or 4 pieces. Place the slices in a colander or on a plate and sprinkle them with salt and leave to stand for 20 minutes. Wash and pat dry.

Peel and chop the onions.

In a large bowl beat the eggs, season and add half of the liquid saffron, stir and set to one side.

COOKING

You need a large non-stick frying pan for *kookoo* as it needs to be turned upside down at the end. For this amount of mixture I usually use a 35 cm/14 inch pan.

Heat 4 tablespoons of oil and fry the chopped onions until golden, remove with a slotted spoon and set to one side. Then fry the aubergine slices on both sides to a golden colour, adding more oil if necessary. Remove with a slotted spoon and place on paper kitchen towel to absorb the extra oil. With a fork chop the slices into small pieces; they should not be completely mashed.

Add the fried onions and the aubergine to the beaten egg and saffron mixture; add the flour, bicarbonate of soda, the rest of liquid saffron and season with salt and pepper. Mix well.

Wipe your frying pan clean. Now melt the butter and 2 tablespoons of oil in the non-stick frying pan. When hot, add the egg mixture; use a wooden spatula to spread the mixture evenly in the pan. Cover the pan with a lid, reduce to a low heat and cook for approximately 35–40 minutes.

NOTE *Kookoo* needs to be cooked very slowly, and should rise to look like a cake.

TO SERVE

Place a large flat dish over the pan and flip the *kookoo* over into it, so that the fried side is up.

Sprinkle the top of the *kookoo* with a mixture of chopped parsley and herbs or even a little finely chopped red chilli. This *kookoo* needs a side plate of yogurt mixed with shallots or cucumber (see pp. 190, 192), and perhaps a pickle or tomato salad. The side dishes are essential as they enhance the flavour of the *kookoo*.

Potato omelette

Kookoo-ye seebzamini

SERVES 4
PREPARATION about 15–20
  minutes
COOKING about 20 minutes

INGREDIENTS

500 g/1 lb 2 oz potatoes
6 eggs
2 medium onions
1 tablespoon plain flour
1 teaspoon bicarbonate of soda
½ teaspoon turmeric
2 dessertspoons liquid saffron
  (*see* INGREDIENTS)
30 g/1 oz butter
2 tablespoons vegetable oil
vegetable oil for frying onion
salt and pepper

Potato is a relatively recent arrival in the Persian kitchen. It was apparently introduced to the south of Iran in the early nineteenth century by the British who were based there at the time. However, it soon gained popularity all over the country and is now used in a wide variety of dishes.

Potato *kookoo* can be served as a light vegetarian meal with a side dish of salad, yogurt or pickle. It is easy to prepare and cook.

PREPARATION

Wash and parboil the potatoes in salted water. When cool, peel the potatoes and grate them.

Peel and chop the onions; fry them in 2 tablespoons of vegetable oil until golden, remove and set to one side.

In a large bowl beat the egg and add the flour, turmeric, liquid saffron and bicarbonate of soda; stir well and then add the grated potato and the onions, stirring vigorously for a few minutes so that the mixture is smooth.

COOKING

You need a large non-stick frying pan for *kookoo*. Melt the butter and 2 tablespoons of oil. When sizzling take a heaped tablespoon of the mixture and pour into the frying pan to form a patty about 10 cm/4 inches in size. Repeat until the mix is used up. Reduce the heat to low and let the patties set; this takes around 10–15 minutes on a very low heat. Turn them over and fry the other side for the same amount of time.

Serve the patties hot in a flat dish with side dishes of pickles, chutney and mixed salad.

VARIATION

You can cook this *kookoo* as a whole, by pouring the mixture into the pan in one go. After 30 minutes of cooking on a low heat, flip the *kookoo* upside down onto a flat dish so that the fried side is up. This way it resembles a cake.

Spinach omelette

Narghesi-e esfenaj

SERVES 4
PREPARATION about 10
   minutes
COOKING about 15 minutes

INGREDIENTS

350 g/12 oz fresh spinach
6 eggs
1 medium onion
2 dessertspoons liquid saffron
   (*see* INGREDIENTS)
2 tablespoons vegetable oil
1 tablespoon butter
salt and pepper

This is a light and fresh omelette, ideal as a starter or light lunch. The name of this dish in Persian, *narghesi*, means 'like narcissus'. The allusion is to the traditional presentation of this dish where the fried eggs sit on a bed of green spinach – in the way that a daffodil or narcissus flower has a yellow centre with white petals around it.

I prefer to beat the egg before adding it to the spinach, but you can break the eggs in the pan and leave them whole, if you wish.

PREPARATION AND COOKING

Remove the tough stems and wash the spinach; peel and finely slice the onion. In a large bowl beat the eggs lightly and add the liquid saffron, salt and pepper to taste.

In a large pan cook the spinach for 3–4 minutes only. There is no need to add water as the washed spinach has enough moisture in it already. Make sure not to overcook as the spinach would be discoloured. Remove and let it cool down a little and then roughly chop.

In a non-stick frying pan heat the oil and melt the butter, fry the onion on medium heat until golden, add the cooked chopped spinach, stir-fry for a couple of minutes. Pour the egg mix over the spinach, reduce the heat and cook until the egg is set but not hard (approximately 10 minutes).

Serve in a flat dish. *Narghesi* is delicious with a side dish of yogurt mixed with cucumber or celery, a tomato and onion salad or any kind of pickle.

CHAPTER 5

Rice dishes

RICE has almost a revered place in Persian cuisine; great attention is paid to its preparation, cooking and presentation. A perfectly cooked rice is fragrant with fully stretched grains, fluffy and light. Rice dishes are the centrepiece on the *sofreh* or table, with everything else arranged around them.

When entertaining guests, there are always at least two rice dishes on the table, one plain (*chelo*) and one where rice is mixed with other ingredients (*polo*).

The crust of the rice (*tahdig*), which develops at the bottom of the pan during the steaming process, is another unique feature of the Persian way of cooking rice. The *tahdig*, literally 'the bottom of the pan', can be made with bread, potatoes or a mixture of rice, yogurt and saffron added to the pan before the boiled rice is returned for steaming.

The rice cooked for festive occasions has to be *ghad keshideh* (long-grain); it has to be steamed with a proportional amount of butter and must produce a perfect golden *tahdig*. The grains of well-steamed rice are long, separate but cooked through. It requires mastery, as they say in Iran, to be able to bring out the 'perfume' of the rice during steaming.

Chelo

The different ways of cooking rice

CHELO AND POLO

Rice is first washed and soaked. It is then drained and boiled, using either the traditional or the absorption method described below. The crusty *tahdig* base is prepared, and the rice is then steamed.

KATEH

A variation of the absorption method is used for *kateh*, in which the rice is gathered in the middle of the pan when the water has evaporated, and then steamed on a low heat.

DAMI

Dami or *dampokhtak* is a sticky, clumpy rice dish. The rice is cooked together with other ingredients such as herbs and vegetables. The rice is boiled and then steamed; the end result is a sticky rice.

Cooking rice

The best variety of rice to use is basmati, which is the closest to the famous Persian *dom siah* (black tail) rice.

Almost all rice dishes involve following standard procedures, as described here. Later distinct rice recipes tend to be elaborations on the basis of these conventional methods. It is therefore worth familiarising yourself with this section before moving on. You can choose between the following methods of cooking rice for the recipes described here.

The standard recipe

Soaking and preparation

Allow approximately 150 g/5 oz of rice per person. Place the rice in a large bowl, add enough cold water until the level is 3–4 cm/1½ inches above the rice. Move the grains around the bowl using your hands. Drain the water and repeat the action until the water remains almost clear. Drain and add water as before. Add a tablespoon of salt per 200 g/7 oz of rice and leave to soak for at least a couple of hours. This gets rid of extra starch and makes the rice fluffier when cooked. Drain and wash the rice before boiling.

Choose a suitable pan for the volume of rice. If cooking for four (600 g/1 lb 5 oz of rice), a pan of approximately 25 cm/10 inches diameter and 12–15 cm/5–6 inches deep is adequate.

Boiling the rice

TRADITIONAL METHOD

Fill the pan more than two-thirds with cold water. Add 1 tablespoon of salt per 500 g/1 lb 2 oz rice. Bring to the boil. Add the drained rice to the boiling water. Let it boil. To begin with, you will see individual grains of rice rising to the surface as the water boils. Gradually, more grains come up to the surface with each bubble. In approximately 10 minutes you will see the pattern of bubbles change to waves of rice rising to the top. Count approximately five waves and then remove from the heat. Drain in a large colander. Test a couple of grains for softness: they should be al dente. If too salty, rinse the rice once with cold water. At this stage other ingredients can be added to the rice before steaming (see below).

ABSORPTION METHOD

This method is simpler, but it does require practice to understand when the process is complete.

Pour an equal volume of water to rice into a pan (for example, 1 cup of rice to 1 cup water), add 1 dessertspoon of salt per 500 g/1 lb 2 oz of rice and bring to the boil. Add the rice and oil or butter (depending on the recipe) and cook over a medium heat. Let it cook, bubbling gently, without stirring, until all the water has evaporated. The best indication of this is when small holes start to appear in the surface of the rice. You have left it too late if, when you remove the rice from the pan, *tahdig* (the crust) has started to form. If it has, discard the *tahdig* and continue with the recipe. At this stage you can add other ingredients to the rice before steaming.

Preparing the *tahdig*

Tahdig is a much-loved, delicious and essential accompaniment to rice. If you have tried Persian rice you will appreciate why *tahdig* is so prized by Persians.

A mixture of butter and cooking oil is placed in the pan. This is allowed to sizzle over a medium heat until foaming. The base is then added, followed by the boiled rice.

There are a wide variety of *tahdigs*. Depending on the recipe you can prepare any of the following:

BREAD

Pieces of flatbread – traditionally the thin Persian bread known as *lavash* – are placed at the bottom of the pan, before returning the rice for steaming. You can use any Middle Eastern flatbread or even pitta bread split in half.

POTATO

Potatoes are very popular as the *tahdig* base. They are peeled and sliced thinly, then washed in cold water to remove the starch, dried and placed in the bottom of the pan with some liquid saffron to make them look golden when served.

YOGURT

Plain yogurt (preferably Greek-style) and liquid saffron are mixed with some of the boiled rice and spread at the bottom of the pan. For dishes where the plain rice is mixed with herbs and vegetables it is important to reserve some plain rice and use this for the *tahdig*.

SAFFRON EGG

Plain boiled rice is mixed with 1 beaten egg and some liquid saffron and spread thinly at the bottom.

VEGETABLE

A large lettuce, cabbage or any other leaves and root vegetables can also be used as the base. When using leaves, make sure that the rice is steamed on a very low heat to prevent burning.

Steaming

The steaming process is the same for both the traditional and the absorption method.

Using a wide slotted spoon, gently pile the rice onto the prepared *tahdig*, starting from the middle of the pan. You should end up with a pyramid of rice. Depending on the recipe, when making *polo* – rice mixed with other ingredients such as pulses, berries, dried fruits, herbs, meat or vegetables – you must mix the rice with the ingredients before piling it in the pan for steaming. Drizzle 2 tablespoons of vegetable oil, or 1 of oil and 30 g/1 oz of butter cut into small pieces, over the top of the pyramid.

Wrap the lid in a clean tea towel and jam it on the pan to stop steam escaping as much as possible. Reduce the heat to low, but ensure that steam continues to rise to the top of the pan. On a gas cooker, reduce the heat to a minimum; if necessary, use a diffuser. Leave to steam for 45 to 50 minutes, as the recipe indicates. The lid should be hot to the touch and the tea towel should be moist with the steam.

Serving

Before serving, dip the bottom of the pan in cold water by standing it in approximately 5 cm/2 inches of cold water in a sink for a couple of minutes. This helps to separate the *tahdig* from the bottom of the pan. Using a slotted server, spoon the rice onto a flat serving dish. Fluff the rice as you do so. Take care not to break the grains.

Remove the *tahdig* in pieces and place around the rice or serve them separately (see individual recipes).

Kateh

This is similar to the absorption method, with the difference that you do not empty the rice after the water is evaporated.

Prepare the rice in the normal way. Drain the rice and rinse once; pour equal volumes of water and rice into a pan (1 cup of rice requires 1 cup of water), add 1 dessertspoon of salt per 500 g/1 lb 2 oz of rice and bring to the boil. Add the rice and some oil or butter (as the recipe indicates) and cook over a medium heat. Let it cook gently until all the water has been absorbed, and small holes start to appear in the surface of the rice.

Reduce the heat to low. At this stage add the other ingredients, depending on the recipe; mix carefully in the pan with a slotted spoon and drizzle oil or a mixture of oil and butter over the rice. Wrap the lid in a clean tea towel and jam it on the pan to stop steam escaping as much as possible. Steam in the usual way over low heat.

Dami

This a sticky rice. Soak the rice as above. Drain it and rinse. Pour into a pan. Add twice the volume of water to the volume of rice. Add the other ingredients according to the recipe, 1 dessertspoon of salt per 500 g/1 lb 2 oz of rice, and oil and cook over a medium heat. You will notice that the rice is much more glutinous. When the water is completely absorbed, steam by reducing the heat to low and put a tea towel wrapped lid on the pan. Let it cook for 40 to 45 minutes.

Tahdig of *ghiemeh polo*

Cabbage and raisin rice

Kalam polo ba keshmesh va advieh

In Iran, cabbage is used mainly as an ingredient with rice. There are different versions of cabbage rice. In *New Persian Cooking* I presented the recipe that my aunt used to cook, which comes from Shiraz, in the south, where I grew up. In that version the fresh aromatic herbs mixed with dill dominate the smell and flavour of the cabbage.

This recipe does not contain herbs. The addition of sultanas (or raisins) with sweet spices like cinnamon generates a completely different taste. White cabbage is most suitable for this recipe but any type that shreds easily can be used.

PREPARATION

Wash the rice and soak for a couple of hours (see STANDARD RECIPE).

Remove four or five of the larger outer leaves of the cabbage and set to one side to use for the *tahdig* (you can make other types of *tahdig*; see above). Cut the cabbage into quarters and cut out the central hard stalk; you should end up with approximately 450 g of tender cabbage leaves. Shred the leaves into 1 cm/½ inch strips.

Peel and chop the onion.

COOKING

In a large frying pan heat 2 tablespoons of vegetable oil and a tablespoon of butter and fry the onion until golden. Add the shredded cabbage, sultanas, turmeric, *advieh*, pepper and 1 dessertspoon of salt and fry for 5–8 minutes. Set to one side.

SERVES 4
PREPARATION about 15 minutes plus soaking
COOKING about 1¼ hours

INGREDIENTS

500 g/1 lb 2 oz basmati rice
500 g/1 lb 2 oz white cabbage
100 g/3½ oz sultanas (or raisins)
1 medium onion
2 tablespoons vegetable oil
50 g/2 oz butter
1 teaspoons turmeric
2 teaspoons rice spice (*advieh*) (see INGREDIENTS).
4 dessertspoons liquid saffron (see INGREDIENTS)
black pepper to taste
450 ml/15 fl oz water
salt

In a heavy-based saucepan large enough to accommodate all the ingredients, bring the water to the boil. Drain the rice and add to the pan, with 1 dessertspoon of salt. Using the absorption method, cook until the water is absorbed and you can see holes appearing on the surface of the rice. Turn the rice out into a large bowl.

Mix the fried cabbage and sultanas and 2 tablespoons of saffron liquid with the rice, making sure the ingredients are evenly blended.

Return the saucepan to the heat. Add the remaining 1 tablespoon of oil and 20 g/¾ oz of the butter and heat until foaming. Line the bottom of the pan with the cabbage leaves (if you are using potato slices or other type of *tahdig*, arrange them to cover the bottom of the pan).

Gently pile the rice and cabbage mixture into the pan, starting in the middle. Try to keep the pile away from the sides as much as possible. Cut the remaining butter into small pieces and dot over the rice. Wrap the lid in a clean tea towel and place it on the pan. Reduce the heat to a minimum and let the rice steam for 50 minutes to 1 hour.

When the rice is ready, stand the pan in cold water to help loosen the *tahdig*. Serve the rice onto a large shallow dish, fluffing it as you do so. Sprinkle the remaining liquid saffron on top.

Cut the crispy *tahdig* into small portions and arrange on a separate plate.

This rice dish goes well with miniature meatballs (see the recipe in *New Persian Cooking*; you can mix the meatballs into the rice to create a variation on the dish), roast lamb or chicken. Serve with a side dish of herbs (*sabzi khordan*) or a mixed salad.

Jewelled rice

Morassa polo

The colourful and fragrant rice dishes that are customarily made for wedding and festivities are called *morassa polo*, meaning jewelled rice. The rice is cooked with liquid saffron mixed with ruby-colour barberries, orange and carrot juliennes, pistachio and almond slivers – indeed resembling scattered jewels.

There are different versions of *morassa polo*, some more ornate and complicated than others. I have included three different versions in this book. This version is more elaborate and closer to the traditional recipe.

PREPARATION

Wash the rice and soak for a couple of hours (see STANDARD RECIPE).

Using a small sharp knife or a peeler, peel the oranges, trimming away as much of the white pith as possible. Cut the peel into uniform juliennes. To extract the bitterness of the orange peel, place it in a small saucepan, add cold water and bring to the boil. Remove from the heat and drain in a sieve. Taste the peel and repeat the blanching if necessary. Drain the peel and set to one side.

Peel the carrots and cut them into juliennes as well. Spread the barberries on a plate and pick them over; discard any stones (sometimes hidden among the berries), pinch off any stalks and wash them thoroughly and drain in a sieve.

SERVES 4
PREPARATION about 25–30 minutes plus soaking
COOKING about 1 hour to 1 hour and 10 minutes.

INGREDIENTS

500 g/1 lb 2 oz basmati rice
2 oranges (preferably unwaxed; use Seville oranges if available)
500 ml/1 pt cold water
200 g/7 oz caster sugar
100 ml/3½ fl oz liquid saffron (*see* INGREDIENTS)
50 g/2 oz pistachio slivers
50 g/2 oz flaked almonds
50 g/2 oz barberries (*zereshk*)
3 large carrots
6 tablespoons vegetable oil
50 g/2 oz butter
salt

GARNISH (OPTIONAL)

20 g/¾ oz pistachio slivers
20 g/¾ oz flaked almonds
1 tablespoon butter
1½ tablespoons liquid saffron

COOKING

Put 100 ml/3½ fl oz of water, the sugar and 3 tablespoons of liquid saffron in a small saucepan. Put on a low heat and let the sugar dissolve.

Add the pistachios, almonds and blanched orange peel. Mix thoroughly and bring to the boil. As soon as the mixture starts bubbling, remove from the heat and set to one side. The mixture should have the consistency of thick syrup and have the colour and scent of saffron. In a frying pan, melt 1 tablespoon of butter with a teaspoon of oil and fry the carrot juliennes on medium heat for 10 minutes, add a tablespoon of liquid saffron and set to one side.

Fry the barberries, in a tablespoon of oil, gently over medium heat until glowing, remove and mix them with the fried carrots.

Put 500 ml/a scant pint of water in a large heavy-based saucepan and bring to the boil. Add 2 tablespoons of liquid saffron and 1 dessertspoon of salt. Drain the rice and add to the pan. Bring back to the boil and then simmer until all the water has been absorbed and holes appear on the surface of the rice.

Tip the rice into a large shallow bowl. Set to one side 2 tablespoons of plain rice for the *tahdig*. Return the pan to the heat. Put 3 tablespoons of oil and a tablespoon of liquid saffron into the pan on a medium heat until sizzling. Sprinkle over the bottom of the pan the rice you have set to one side for the *tahdig*. Using a slotted spoon, layer in the nut and peel mixture with the rice, alternating with the barberry and carrot mix, creating layers of rice with the mixtures in the middle of the pan piling up to the top.

Cut the butter into small pieces and dot over the rice. Wrap the lid in a clean tea towel and place firmly on the pan. Reduce the heat to a minimum (on a gas cooker, use a heat diffuser if necessary) and steam for 45–50 minutes.

When the rice is ready, stand the pan in 5 cm/2 inches of cold water for 1–2 minutes to loosen the crispy *tahdig*. Serve out the rice onto a shallow dish, fluffing it with a slotted spoon. For the garnish, melt the butter and stir-fry the slivers of pistachio and almond for 1 minute, add the liquid saffron. Pour on top of the rice.

For the *tahdig*, remove the crispy layer from the pan, cut into small pieces and serve on a separate plate.

This dish has layers of aroma with saffron dominant; it therefore needs little enhancement. Traditionally it is served with saffron-tinged lemon chicken or lamb and split peas (*khoresh-e gheimeh*; see the recipe in *New Persian Cooking*).

Tahdig of *morassa polo*

Saffron jewelled rice

Shirin polo

This is a simpler version of jewelled rice, which contains only pistachio and almond slivers along with the orange juliennes.

PREPARATION

Wash the rice and soak in salted cold water for a couple of hours (see STANDARD RECIPE).

Using a small sharp knife or a peeler, peel the oranges, trimming away as much pith as possible. Cut the peel into juliennes. Place the orange juliennes in a small saucepan of water and bring to the boil. Remove from the heat and drain in a sieve. Taste for bitterness and repeat the blanching if necessary. Drain and set to one side.

COOKING

Put 125 ml/4 fl oz of water, all the sugar and 3 tablespoons of liquid saffron in a small saucepan. Put on a low heat and let the sugar dissolve.

Add the pistachios, almonds and blanched orange peel. Mix thoroughly and bring to the boil. As soon as the mixture starts bubbling, remove from the heat and set to one side. The mixture should have the consistency of thick syrup and the colour and scent of saffron. Add more liquid saffron if needed.

Pour 2 tablespoons of liquid saffron and 3 tablespoons of oil into a small pan, bring to the boil and set to one side.

Put 550 ml/1 pint water in a large heavy-based saucepan and bring to the boil. Add 2 tablespoons of liquid saffron and 1 dessertspoon of salt. Drain the rice and add to the pan.

SERVES 4–6
PREPARATION about 25 minutes plus soaking
COOKING about 1 hour

INGREDIENTS

600 g/1 lb 5 oz basmati rice
1 or 2 oranges (preferably unwaxed)
750 ml/1¼ pints cold water
250 g/9 oz caster sugar
100 ml/3½ fl oz liquid saffron (*see* INGREDIENTS)
50 g/2 oz pistachio slivers
50 g/2 oz flaked almonds
6 tablespoons vegetable oil
50 g/2 oz butter
salt

Bring back to the boil and then simmer until all the water has been absorbed and holes appear on the surface of the rice.

Tip the rice into a shallow bowl. Set to one side 2 tablespoons of plain rice for the *tahdig*. Set to one side 1 tablespoon of the nut and peel mixture for the garnish. Mix the rest of the nut and peel mixture thoroughly with the rice.

Return the pan to the heat. Put the remaining oil into the pan on a medium heat until sizzling. Sprinkle the rice you have set to one side for the *tahdig* at the bottom of the pan. With a slotted spoon, pile the rice and nut mixture in the middle of the pan. Cut the butter into small pieces and dot over the rice. Wrap the lid in a clean tea towel and place firmly on the pan. Reduce the heat to a minimum (on a gas cooker, reduce the heat to a minimum and use a heat diffuser if necessary) and steam for 45–50 minutes.

When the rice is ready, stand the pan in 5 cm/2 inches of cold water for 1–2 minutes to loosen the crispy *tahdig*. Serve the rice onto a shallow dish, fluffing the rice with a slotted spoon. Pour the reserved nuts and peel mixture on top as garnish. Drizzle the oil and saffron mixture over the garnished rice. Remove the *tahdig* from the pan, cut into small pieces and serve on a separate plate.

A simple green leaf salad with a lemon and olive oil dressing complements the intense taste of this rice dish.

Saffron jewelled rice with sultana, chestnut, figs, almond, pistachio and dates

Morassa polo

SERVES 4
PREPARATION about 15
   minutes plus soaking
COOKING about 1 hour

INGREDIENTS

400 g/14 oz basmati rice
400 ml/14 fl oz water
100 ml/3½ fl oz liquid saffron
   (*see* INGREDIENTS)
100 g/3½ oz sultanas
40 g/1½ oz chopped chestnuts
30 g/1 oz chopped dried figs
30 g/1 oz chopped dates
40 g/1½ oz almond flakes
30 g/1 oz pistachio slivers
1 medium onion
8–10 tablespoons vegetable oil
50 g/2 oz butter
salt

Chestnuts are not a very common ingredient in Persian cooking; nevertheless they work very well combined with dried fruits in this very old recipe. This is a wonderful vegetarian rice dish. It can also be served with shredded chicken breast for non-vegetarians.

PREPARATION

Wash the rice repeatedly in plenty of cold water. Once clean, soak it in a bowl of cold salted water (see STANDARD RECIPE).

Ready-prepared chestnuts in packets can be bought in good supermarkets. Chop the chestnuts roughly with a sharp knife to end up with pieces measuring about 1 cm/½ inch. Do the same for the dates and the dried figs. Peel the onion and chop it finely.

COOKING

In a frying pan heat 4 tablespoons of oil and fry the onion. When golden add the sultanas, stir and then add the mixture of chopped chestnuts, figs and dates. Fry for a couple of minutes; add 3 teaspoons of liquid saffron and set to one side.

In another small frying pan, lightly fry the almond flakes and the pistachio slivers in a tablespoon of oil, mix in 2 teaspoons of liquid saffron.

For this rice I prefer to use the absorption method (see STANDARD RECIPE); however the traditional recipe can also be used. In a heavy-based saucepan, larger than you would use for plain rice, boil the water and add 2 tablespoons of liquid saffron. Drain the rice and add to the pan. Add 1 dessertspoon of salt and adjust seasoning. Bring to the boil and let the rice cook until all the water is evaporated and holes appear on the surface.

Once the water has evaporated, pour the rice into a shallow bowl. Set to one side 1 tablespoon of the mixture of almond and pistachio, 1 tablespoon of chestnut and fig mixture for the garnish and a couple of tablespoons of plain rice. Blend the rest of the chestnut mixture and the almond and pistachio mix thoroughly with the rice.

Pour the rest of the oil into the pan to cover the bottom. Heat over a medium heat until sizzling and then line the bottom of the pan with the boiled rice you have set to one side to make the *tahdig* (following the STANDARD RECIPE). Spoon the rice mixture with a slotted spoon into the middle of the pan, piling it into a pyramid. Cut the butter into small pieces and dot on the rice. Wrap the lid in a tea towel and fix firmly onto the pan. Lower the heat to a minimum and allow to steam for 30 minutes to 1 hour.

When the time is up, stand the pan in about 5 cm/2 inches of cold water for a couple of minutes and remove. Take the lid off and fluff the rice as you spoon it onto a flat serving dish. Pour the reserved nut mixture on top as garnish. Drizzle the oil and saffron mixture over the garnished rice. Separate the crispy layer of the *tahdig* and cut it into small pieces. Arrange on a separate plate.

Serve with any chicken dish.

This is a rich rice dish which needs a refreshing side dish like yogurt or a citrus green salad.

Saffron carrot rice with orange juliennes and pistachio

Haveej polo

This is a colourful and fragrant rice dish which goes well with poultry or lamb.

Although an easy dish to make, it needs attention to detail for the outcome to be perfect.

PREPARATION

Wash the rice repeatedly in plenty of cold water. Once clean, soak it in a bowl of cold salted water for a couple of hours (see STANDARD RECIPE).

To prepare the orange juliennes, peel the oranges and cut away as much of the white pith as possible. Cut the peel into juliennes.

To extract the bitterness of the orange peel, take a small saucepan, half fill it with water, put the orange peel juliennes into the pan and bring to the boil. Remove from the heat and drain into a sieve. Taste the peel and repeat the above if needed. Drain the peel and set to one side.

Wash and peel the carrots and slice them into slivers the size of matchsticks (you can use a mandolin for this).

COOKING

In a small saucepan, pour ½ cup of water, all the sugar and 3 tablespoons of liquid saffron. Put on a low heat and allow the sugar to dissolve. Add the pistachio and orange peel. Mix thoroughly and bring to the boil. As soon as the mixture starts bubbling, remove from the heat and set to one side. The mixture should have the consistency of a thick syrup and have the colour and scent of saffron. Add more saffron if needed.

SERVES 4–6
PREPARATION about 20 minutes plus soaking time
COOKING about 1 hour

INGREDIENTS

500 g/1 lb 2 oz basmati rice
500 g/1 lb 2 oz carrot juliennes
50 g/2 oz pistachio slivers
40 g/1½ oz orange peel juliennes
200 g/7 oz sugar
6 tablespoons vegetable oil
50 g/2 oz butter
4 tablespoons liquid saffron (*see* INGREDIENTS)
500 ml/1 pint water
salt

Heat half of the oil in a frying pan, fry the carrot slivers for 5 minutes, add ½ cup of water mixed with 2 teaspoons of saffron and gently cook for 10 minutes. Remove from the heat and add the syrup mix of orange and pistachio. Stir well and set to one side.

In a heavy-based saucepan large enough to accommodate all the ingredients, boil the water and add 1 dessertspoon of liquid saffron. Drain the rice and add to the pan. Add salt and adjust the seasoning. Bring to the boil and let it cook until all the water has evaporated and holes appear on the surface of the rice.

Once the water has evaporated pour the rice into a shallow bowl. Set to one side 1 tablespoon of the carrot, nut and peel mixture for the garnish and a couple of tablespoons of plain rice. Mix the rest of the nuts and peel mixture thoroughly with the rice.

Pour the rest of the oil into the pan to cover the bottom. Heat over a medium heat until sizzling and then line the bottom of the pan with the boiled rice you have set to one side to make the *tahdig* (following the STANDARD RECIPE). Spoon the rice mixture with a slotted spoon into the middle of the pan, piling it into a pyramid. Cut the butter into small pieces and dot on the rice. Wrap the lid in a tea towel and fix firmly onto the pan. Lower the heat to minimum (make sure the heat is very low as the sugary rice can easily burn) and allow to steam for 45–50 minutes.

When the time is up, stand the pan in 5 cm/2 inches of cold water for a couple of minutes. Remove, take the lid off and fluff the rice as you spoon it onto a flat serving dish. Pour the reserved nut and peel mixture on top as garnish. Drizzle the oil and saffron mixture over the garnished rice. Separate the crispy *tahdig* layer and cut it into small pieces; arrange on a separate plate.

SERVING SUGGESTIONS

You can serve this rice with shredded chicken breast spread on top of the rice.

RECIPE FOR CHICKEN BREASTS

You can cook the chicken breasts in any way you like. The following is a suggestion. In a small saucepan, heat 2 table-spoonsful of vegetable oil. Peel a medium onion and cut into 4 wedges. Wash 2 chicken breast fillets, dry them. Place the onions and the chicken breast in the pan, fry until golden. Add 2 cups of water and 2 tablespoons of lemon juice, bring to the boil. Reduce the heat and allow to simmer for 30–40 minutes. Add 2 teaspoons of liquid saffron, stir and set to one side. Shred the breasts and place on top of the rice.

Noodle rice

Reshteh polo

SERVES 4–6
PREPARATION about 10
minutes plus soaking
COOKING about 1 hour and 10
minutes

INGREDIENTS

500 g/1 lb 2 oz basmati rice
250 g/9 oz thin wheat noodles
    (use ready-made noodles,
    available from Persian or
    Middle Eastern shops)
3 medium onions
250 g/9 oz raisins
250 g/9 oz dates
1 teaspoon turmeric
1 teaspoon cumin powder
1 teaspoon cinnamon
3 tablespoons liquid saffron
    (*see* INGREDIENTS)
salt and pepper
4 tablespoons vegetable oil
30 g/1 oz butter
4–5 pieces of flatbread for the
    tahdig
salt

Noodles have been used in Persian cooking for many centuries. There are many recipes in the old cookbooks that add spherical-shaped noodles to *aashes* and soups.

Nowadays noodles are mainly used in noodle *aash* (see p. 130) and in this rice dish.

In Persian, *reshteh* means 'thread'. This dish comes from the province of Kermanshah in the west of Iran, where it is made on the eve of the New Year (*Norouz*), as the threads direct one towards making the right decisions in the year to come. I am indebted to my friend Sheila, who is a brilliant cook, for giving me this recipe.

PREPARATION

Wash the rice several times and soak in salted water for a couple of hours (see STANDARD RECIPE).

Peel and chop the onions finely. Chop the dates into 1 cm/½ inch pieces.

COOKING

In a large frying pan heat 2 tablespoons of oil and fry the onions until golden. Add the dates and stir-fry for a couple of minutes. Add the raisins, turmeric, cinnamon, cumin and 1 tablespoon of liquid saffron, salt and pepper to taste. Fry for a further 2–3 minutes, remove from the heat and set to one side.

Toast the noodles (you can break them in half) lightly in a dry frying pan until lightly golden and crispy (about 3–4 minutes) then set to one side.

Cook the rice according to the traditional method (see standard recipe). Fill a large saucepan three-quarters full with water, add 2 tablespoons of salt and bring to the boil. Drain the rice and add to the boiling water. When you see waves of rice coming to the surface (approximately 5–6 minutes) add the toasted noodles, allow to boil until you have counted 4–5 waves of rice coming to the surface. Drain the noodle and rice mix in a large colander. Fold in half of the fried onion, raisins and date mix into the rice, carefully stir to mix all the ingredients with the rice. Return the pan to the heat; when hot, add 2 tablespoons of oil, arrange the bread pieces at the bottom and reduce the heat.

Pile up the rice mix in the middle of the pan, add 1 tablespoon of butter. Cover with the lid, lower the heat (using a diffuser if necessary) and steam the rice for 50 minutes to 1 hour.

Remove from the heat and place the pan in 5 cm/2 inches of cold water for a couple of minutes to loosen the *tahdig*. Using a large slotted serving spoon, place the rice in a flat dish, fluffing it as you do so. Warm up the fried mix of onions, raisins and dates and pour over the rice; sprinkle the remaining liquid saffron over.

Reshteh polo is traditionally served with chicken. It is delicious with a side dish of pickle and fresh herbs (*sabzi khordan*).

Biryani from Bushehr

Beriani Bushehri

Biryani, from the Persian word *beriani*, means grilling on the fire. The origin goes back to the court of Mughul kings in India. There are many versions from different parts of India.

My recipe is a variation of the biryani that I used to have in my grandfather's house in Bushehr, by the Persian Gulf.

PREPARATION

Wash the rice several times and soak in salted water for a couple of hours (see STANDARD RECIPE).

Cut the chicken breasts into 3 cm/1 inch-wide strips.

Grate the ginger.

Finely chop the onion and the garlic.

Soak the raisins for 20–30 minutes in a cup of hot water, with a teaspoon of liquid saffron

COOKING

Pour 400 ml/14 fl oz of water into a heavy-based saucepan and bring to the boil. Drain the rice and add to the boiling water with 1 dessertspoon of salt and half of the butter and the vegetable oil. Simmer on a medium heat until the water has evaporated (about 10 minutes) and holes start to appear on the surface. Empty the rice into a colander and set to one side.

In a large frying pan fry the onions until golden, add the garlic, ginger and chicken strips and stir-fry for 3–4 minutes. Add the rest of the spices, stir well. Add the chicken stock and simmer for 10–15 minutes. The sauce should be thick at this stage.

SERVES 4
PREPARATION about 10 minutes plus soaking
COOKING about 45–50 minutes

INGREDIENTS

400 g/14 oz basmati rice
4 chicken breasts (skinless)
1 medium onion
6 cloves of garlic
3 teaspoons grated fresh root ginger
2 teaspoons chilli powder
1 teaspoon ground cumin
2 teaspoons ground coriander/ cilantro
1 teaspoon ground cinnamon
2 cardamom pods
1 teaspoon turmeric
4 dessertspoons liquid saffron (*see* INGREDIENTS)
250 g/9 oz cups of yogurt
1 tablespoon sugar
150 g/5 oz raisins
4 tablespoons vegetable oil
30 g/1 oz butter
150 ml/5 fl oz chicken stock
salt

GARNISH

30 g/1 oz flaked almonds
1 medium onion, finely chopped
2 teaspoons liquid saffron

Remove from the heat and fold in the yogurt, the boiled rice and the raisins. Stir to mix the ingredients. Heat 2 tablespoons of the oil in the saucepan, return the mixture to the pan, reduce the heat to minimum and steam for 30 minutes. (A thin *tahdig* might form, which can be served separately.)

For the garnish, heat 2 tablespoons of the oil and a tablespoon of butter in a frying pan and fry the onion until golden brown, add the almond flakes, stir, remove from the heat and add the saffron.

Serve the *beriani* in large shallow dish and pour the garnish all over.

Beriani goes well with any hot chutney and a side dish of yogurt.

Fish and dill *dami* rice

Lakh lakh

SERVES 4
PREPARATION about 15–20
minutes plus soaking
COOKING about 1 hour

INGREDIENTS

500 g/1 lb 2 oz chunky fish
    fillets (e.g. haddock or cod)
500 g/1 lb 2 oz basmati rice
2 large onions
100 g/3½ oz fresh dill
100 g/3½ oz fresh coriander
1 teaspoon turmeric
6 cloves of garlic
1–2 hot chillies
1 teaspoon dried lime powder
1 teaspoon chilli flakes
6 tablespoons vegetable oil
30 g/1 oz butter
1½ litres/2½ pints water
salt and pepper

The name of this dish apparently comes from an Arabic word meaning 'fragrant'. It is a wonderfully aromatic rice steamed with dill, coriander, garlic and fish. In Bushehr, on the Persian Gulf, *lakh lakh* is especially popular with the poor, because the ingredients are cheap and readily available. It is a delicious and nutritious dish with a good balance of protein, carbohydrate and fresh herbs.

PREPARATION

Wash the rice and soak it in cold salted water for a couple of hours (see STANDARD RECIPE).

Wash the dill and the coriander, discard any tough stems and dry with paper kitchen towel or in a salad crisper. With a sharp wide-bladed knife chop them finely

Peel and chop the onions and the garlic. Chop the chillies.

Wash the fish fillets and cut them into 3–4 cm/1½ inch cubes; sprinkle the pieces with salt and pepper, set to one side.

COOKING

In a large heavy-based saucepan, heat 4 tablespoons of the oil and fry the onions until golden brown, add ½ teaspoon of turmeric, the garlic and the chillies and stir-fry for a couple of minutes.

With a slotted spoon remove half of the fried mix and set to one side. Add the rice, dill, coriander and 1 teaspoon of turmeric to the same pan. Stir to mix the rice with the other ingredients. Pour the water into the pan, add 1 dessertspoon of salt and boil gently on a medium heat until the water

has been absorbed. Wrap the lid in a tea towel and jam it firmly onto the pan. Reduce the heat to low and cook for 30 minutes. Then add the fish to the pan, stir gently with a large spoon to mix with the rice, add the butter and the rest of the oil. Replace the lid and cook for a further 20 minutes. Dip the bottom of the pan in cold water before serving to separate any crust.

Serve in a flat dish, pour the saved fried onions on the top, sprinkle with chilli flakes and the dried lime powder.

Lakh lakh is delicious with garlic pickle (see p. 198) and a mixed salad of red onions, lettuce and cherry tomatoes dressed with olive oil and lemon.

Seer torshi, garlic pickle

Potato dill rice from Shiraz

Shirazi seebzamini polo

Shiraz, in the south of Iran, is known as the city of poets and rose gardens. Herb rice combined with dill and vegetables such as cabbage, potato or green beans are very popular and suitable for the hot and dry summer months in Shiraz.

This recipe is an adaptation of the potato rice cooked by my aunt.

Dill is a very refreshing addition to the mixture of rice and potatoes, which can otherwise be heavy. The garnish of fried onions adds another layer of taste to this dish.

PREPARATION

Measure, wash and soak the rice in cold salted water (see STANDARD RECIPE).

Wash the dill and use a salad crisper to get rid of the excess water. Pinch off and keep all the fresh young leaves and tender stalks and discard the rest. Take a sharp wide-bladed knife and finely chop.

Peel the potatoes and dice them into 2 cm/¾ inch wedges (wash and keep in cold water to prevent discoloration).

Peel and finely chop the onion and the garlic.

COOKING

In a large frying pan, fry the onion in 2 tablespoons of vegetable oil and 20 g/¾ oz of butter until golden. Remove with a slotted spoon and set to one side. In the same frying pan add 2 tablespoons of oil and fry the potatoes on a gentle heat until they are semi-soft and golden (about 10 minutes). Return the onion to the pan, add 1 teaspoon of turmeric and stir-fry for 1 minute. Remove from the heat and add the dill

SERVES 4
PREPARATION about 20 minutes plus soaking
COOKING 1¼ hours

INGREDIENTS
400 g/14 oz basmati rice
400 ml/14 fl oz water
150 g/5 oz fresh dill
1 large onion
4 cloves of garlic
2 medium potatoes (any type)
2 teaspoons turmeric
100 g/3½ oz butter
3 tablespoons vegetable oil
salt

and chopped garlic and salt to taste. Stir thoroughly and set to one side.

In a heavy-based saucepan (large enough to accommodate all the ingredients), boil the water and add ½ teaspoon of turmeric. Add the rice and 1 dessertspoon of salt. Let the rice cook in the water until the water is absorbed and you can see holes appearing on the surface of the rice, which has taken the yellow colour of the turmeric. Turn the rice out into a large bowl.

Mix the potatoes and dill with the rice. Make sure the potatoes and herb mix is evenly distributed in the rice.

Return the saucepan to the heat. Pour the rest of the oil and 20 g/¾ oz of butter into the pan and heat until foaming. You can use any of the *tahdigs* described in the standard *tahdig* preparation for this rice

Pile the rice in the middle and form it into a pyramid. Cut the butter into small pieces and dot on the top of the rice. Wrap the lid in a tea towel and jam it firmly onto the pan. Lower the heat to minimum and let the rice steam for 50 minutes to 1 hour.

For the onion garnish, fry the onions in 3 tablespoons of oil until golden brown, add ½ teaspoon of turmeric and stir-fry for 1 minute. Take the onion out of the pan with a slotted spoon and place on paper kitchen towel to remove excess oil.

Take the pan off the heat and place it in 5 cm/2 inches of cold water for a couple of minutes to loosen the *tahdig*. Serve the rice onto a large shallow platter, fluffing it as you do so. Spread the fried onions on top of the rice. Cut the crispy *tahdig* into small portions and arrange on a separate plate.

Seebzamini polo is delicious with lamb or chicken dishes; it is equally enjoyable as a vegetarian dish.

Serve it with a hot pickle and a tomato and onion salad.

Rice with lamb, split peas and spices with side dishes

Gheimeh polo ba advieh

This dish combines one of the most loved and popular *khoreshes*, *khoresh-e gheimeh* (lamb and split pea), with another favourite, *chelo* (plain) rice.

Gheimeh is a delicious, flavoursome *khoresh* which is easy to make and good value for money. It is therefore suitable for any occasion from festive to everyday meal. The meat is cut into small pieces (hence the name *gheimeh*, which in Farsi means 'small bits'), fried with onions, flavoured with turmeric, dried lime, saffron and other spices, combined with split peas, to create a perfect balance.

The dish is very popular all over Iran and can be cooked all year round.

Gheimeh polo reminds me of my student days in Shiraz: we used to frequent a little restaurant that served it as its signature dish, accompanied by a number of well-chosen side dishes.

PREPARATION

Wash and soak the split peas in cold water for at least 30 minutes or overnight (follow the instructions on the packet).

Peel and chop the onions. Wash and dry the dried limes and pierce with a fork.

Wash and dry the lamb, trim off any skin and fat and cut the meat into 1 cm/½ inch cubes.

Wash the rice and soak in cold salted water (see STANDARD RECIPE).

SERVES 4–6

PREPARATION about 40–45 minute plus soaking (including preparation of side dishes)

COOKING about 2½ hours

INGREDIENTS

FOR THE GHEIMEH

500 g/1 lb 2 oz lean leg of lamb (off the bone)
150 g/5 oz split peas
1 medium onion
3 dried limes
4 tablespoons vegetable oil
1 teaspoon turmeric
1 teaspoon powdered dried lime (*see* INGREDIENTS)
2 teaspoons cinnamon
3 tablespoons liquid saffron (*see* INGREDIENTS)
1 tablespoon tomato purée/ tomato paste
2 tablespoons lemon juice
750 ml/1¼ pints hot water

FOR THE RICE

350 g/12 oz basmati rice
50 g/2 oz butter
4 tablespoons vegetable oil
400 ml/14 fl oz water
salt

COOKING

Heat 2 tablespoons of vegetable oil in a medium-sized heavy-based saucepan. Fry the onion until golden.

Add the lamb, turmeric, lime powder, whole dried limes, cinnamon, salt and pepper. Stir well and fry until the meat is golden brown all over.

Add the hot water and reduce the heat. Cover with a lid and simmer on a low heat until the meat is nearly cooked (approximately 45–50 minutes).

Drain the split peas and add to the pan. Cover and cook on a low heat for about 30 minutes or until the split peas are cooked: they should be soft while still retaining their shape. Add a small amount of boiling water if the mixture looks dry.

Add the tomato purée/tomato paste and lemon juice, 2 dessertspoons of liquid saffron and cook for a further 10 minutes on a low heat. Set to one side.

To cook the rice, pour 400 ml/14 fl oz of water into a heavy-based saucepan and bring to the boil. Drain the rice and add to the boiling water with 1 dessertspoon of salt, 50 g/2 oz of butter and 3 tablespoons of oil. Leave to simmer uncovered, on a medium heat, until all the water has been absorbed and holes start to appear on the surface of the rice (approximately 10 minutes).

Tip the rice into a shallow dish. To make a rice *tahdig*, set to one side 2 heaped tablespoons of the plain rice. Gently fold 3 tablespoons of the liquid saffron into the rice, making sure the grains of rice are not broken as you mix.

Return the saucepan to the heat. Add 2 tablespoons of vegetable oil and 1 tablespoon of liquid saffron. When it is sizzling, arrange a couple of tablespoons of cooked plain rice in the bottom of the pan (or make another type of *tahdig*).

FOR THE SIDE DISHES

2 large limes
1 orange (or Seville orange)
1 large onion
1 medium red onion
enough vegetable oil to
    deep-fry the onion
garlic pickle (or similar)
300 g/11 oz Greek-style yogurt
2 teaspoons dried mint

Spoon half of the rice into the pan, layer the lamb and split peas mix over the rice and spoon the remaining rice over the mix.

Keep the rice in a pyramid shape and away from the sides of the pan as much as possible. Dot the rest of the butter on top of the rice. Wrap the lid in a clean tea towel and jam it firmly onto the pan. Leave to steam on a low heat (on a gas cooker, reduce the heat to a minimum and use a heat diffuser if necessary) for at least 50 minutes to 1 hour.

When the rice is ready, stand the pan in 5 cm/2 inches of cold water for a few minutes, to help release the bottom layer. Serve the rice in a shallow dish, fluffing it as you spoon it out, blending the layers of lamb and split peas with the rice. Drizzle the remaining liquid saffron over the rice. Detach and break the crispy layer of *tahdig* from the bottom of the pan and serve on a separate plate.

FOR THE SIDE DISHES

The following accompaniments are an essential part of this dish, comprising fried onions, lime and oranges, and garlic pickle (or a similar pickle, such as mango, lime or aubergine), red onions and yogurt (for example, yogurt and wild shallots).

Peel the limes and the orange, removing the pulp and the pips, and dice the flesh into small segments; arrange in a bowl.

Slice the large onion. In a deep frying pan, heat enough oil to deep-fry the onion slices. Take out with a slotted spoon and place on a plate covered with paper kitchen towel to remove excess oil. Allow to cool and arrange in a shallow bowl.

Spoon the pickle from the jar into a small bowl. Finely chop the red onion and place in a small bowl. Choose any yogurt side dish and serve it in a small clear glass bowl.

Side dishes for *gheimeh polo*

Spinach upside-down rice

Tahchin-e esfenaj

Tahchin means literally 'arranged at the bottom', referring to the layering of meat and rice to form a thick *tahdig* (crust) at the bottom of the pan. It is a very popular rice dish which can be made with either lamb or chicken. Some versions contain spinach or aubergine. A good, thick *tahdig* is the distinctive feature of this rice; to obtain that, traditionally the rice is mixed with egg in addition to yogurt.

    Tahchin should preferably be cooked in a non-stick pan, so that it can be served upside down with the golden crust on top like a cake. The classic *tahchin* recipe can be found in *New Persian Cooking*. This version with spinach combines the special flavour of spinach with the delicate aroma of saffron. It is aesthetically pleasing with alternating layers of saffron rice and green spinach.

PREPARATION

Wash the rice several times and soak in cold salted water (see STANDARD RECIPE).

    Wash and trim the lamb, cut into approximately 10 cm/ 4 inch chunks and sprinkle with salt.

    Peel the onions, cut one into 4 pieces and finely chop the other.

    Wash the spinach, discard the tough stems, dry in a salad crisper and chop with a wide-bladed knife.

    Mix the yogurt and 4 tablespoons of liquid saffron and beat the egg into the yogurt, add salt to taste.

SERVES 4–6
PREPARATION about 30 minutes plus soaking
COOKING about 2¼ hours

INGREDIENTS

500 g/1 lb 2 oz basmati rice
750 g/1 lb 10 oz shoulder of lamb (boned)
2 medium onions
2 teaspoons turmeric
6 tablespoons liquid saffron (*see* INGREDIENTS)
300 g/11 oz Greek-style yogurt
750 g/1 lb 10 oz fresh spinach (cooking dramatically reduces the volume)
450 ml/15 fl oz water
250 ml/9 fl oz boiling water
6 tablespoons vegetable oil
30 g/1 oz butter
1 egg
salt

COOKING

Choose a heavy-based saucepan, preferably non-stick and large enough to allow room for all the ingredients to steam well together. Heat 2 tablespoons of oil and lightly fry the onion chunks, add the meat, 1 teaspoon of turmeric, 1 tablespoon of liquid saffron, salt and pepper. Add about 250 ml/9 fl oz of boiling water, stir well, bring back to boil, reduce the heat, cover and allow to simmer for 1–1½ hours. The meat should be almost cooked by this stage.

In a frying pan, heat 2 tablespoons of the oil and fry the chopped onions until golden. Add the chopped spinach and fry for 5–10 minutes. The spinach will shrink in volume considerably. Add the rest of the turmeric, salt and pepper, stir well and remove from the heat. Set to one side to cool.

Make the rice in the same pan that the meat has been cooked in. Take the meat pieces out and put to one side. Add enough cold water to the already existing juices in the pan to end up with a volume of 450 ml/15 fl oz. Add 1 dessertspoon of salt and bring to the boil. Drain the rice and add to the pan with 2 tablespoons of oil and half of the butter and a tablespoon of liquid saffron. Gently simmer on medium heat until the water has evaporated, and small holes start to appear on the surface of the rice. Empty the rice into a large colander or large bowl. Mix the rice with the meat and saffron yogurt mixture, making sure that the meat pieces are coated with yogurt and saffron and evenly distributed.

Return the pan to the heat, add 2 tablespoons of oil and 1 tablespoon of liquid saffron. When hot, place some of the rice and meat mix evenly in the bottom of the pan, reduce the heat to low and add a layer of the spinach and onion mixture. Continue alternating a layer of rice and meat with a layer of spinach to the top, making sure that the spinach layer is distributed thinly and evenly. Add to the pan the rest of the butter, oil and any liquid saffron that is left. Wrap the lid in a tea towel and jam tightly onto the pan. Steam the rice for at least 1–1¼ hours.

Remove from the heat and stand the pan in 2 cm/¾ inch of cold water in the sink for a couple of minutes to loosen the *tahdig*. If you have used a non-stick pan, turn the rice upside down onto a flat dish; alternatively take the lamb pieces out and arrange in a flat serving dish and then spoon the rice over the lamb.

Tahchin is delicious with any pickle or chutney. A tomato and onion salad and fresh herbs (*sabzi khordan*) go well with it.

Tomato, red onion and red pepper salad

Tomato *dami* rice

Dami-e gojehfaranghi

SERVES 4
PREPARATION about 10–15
   minutes plus soaking
COOKING about 1¾ hours

INGREDIENTS

500 g/1 lb 2 oz lean leg of lamb
750 g/1 lb 10 oz fresh tomatoes
   or 500 g/1 lb 2 oz tomato
   passata or 450 g/1 lb can of
   chopped tomatoes
1 medium onion
1 teaspoon turmeric
1 cinnamon stick
1 tablespoon tomato purée
500 g/1 lb 2 oz basmati rice
30 g/1 oz butter
6 tablespoons vegetable oil
salt and pepper

This is a simple but versatile rice dish. It can be cooked either with or without meat, with the addition of potato or not, and made more or less spicy.

In the south they call the dish 'tomato *polo*' and make it hot and spicy without meat. In the north it is often made with meat and sometimes with the addition of potato, when it is called 'Istanbuli *polo*' – because the small potatoes used originally came from Istanbul.

In all cases the rice is cooked in *dami* style (see standard preparation), which means that the rice is cooked in plenty of liquid and is not drained before steaming as in the traditional cooking method. The end result, therefore, is quite moist and sticky, very different from the traditional fluffy long-grain Persian rice. This is a much easier method of cooking rice as it does not need the mastery and experience that are required to make a perfect *ghad keshideh* (long-grain) rice. In Iran they say that if the rice becomes sticky, you know the cook is a novice.

This dish is traditionally cooked with fresh tomatoes but works equally well with canned chopped tomatoes or Italian tomato passata.

This recipe is the tomato *dami* version with meat.

PREPARATION

Wash the rice and soak in cold salted water (see STANDARD RECIPE).

Peel and finely chop the onion.

Wash and trim the lamb by removing the fatty bits, dice into 1 cm/½ inch cubes.

If using fresh tomatoes, place them in boiling water for a few minutes, peel and coarsely chop them.

COOKING

In a medium saucepan heat 2 tablespoons of the oil and fry the onions until golden. Add the diced lamb, turmeric and tomato purée. Fry for approximately 5–8 minutes and then add enough boiling water to half-fill the pan. Bring to the boil, reduce the heat, add the cinnamon stick, salt and pepper to taste, cover and simmer for approximately 1 hour, until the meat is cooked. The remaining sauce should be thick, with little water; reduce if necessary. Remove from the heat and set to one side.

Place the fresh, canned or passata tomatoes in a large heavy-based saucepan, add 500 ml/1 pint of water and mix well (you need to end up with 1 litre/1¾ pints of liquid for 500 g/1 lb 2 oz of rice). Bring to the boil. Drain the soaked rice and add to the pan containing the tomato passata (so it is cooked in the tomato juice) with 2 dessertspoons of salt, 4 tablespoons of vegetable oil and the butter. Reduce the heat to medium and boil the rice until the water has almost evaporated. Stir the rice and tomato mixture, place the meat in the middle of the rice. Wrap the lid in a tea towel, jam firmly onto the pan and steam for 45 minutes.

Before serving, dip the bottom of the pan in cold water to help remove the *tahdig*. The *tahdig* of *dami* is not as crisp as the other *tahdigs*, being softer and thinner; it is nevertheless delicious.

To serve, first take the meat mixture out of the pan and keep warm, then put the rest of the *dami* in a shallow dish, place the meat over the top.

This dish goes well with a side dish of green salad with red onions. In Iran, popular accompaniments are gherkins or garlic pickle.

VEGETARIAN VARIATION WITH POTATO

Peel 300 g/11 oz salad potatoes, cut them into 1 cm/½ inch pieces. Cook the rice the same way as above, but add the potatoes to the boiling tomato mixture together with the rice. Steam for 50 minutes. When serving, you may wish to sprinkle some hot red chilli over the rice.

CHAPTER 6

Appetisers and accompaniments

THE WAY Iranians eat and serve food is very different from the Western tradition. In the West, the table is set and guests are asked to come and sit down to eat. They are then served with the first course or 'starter', then the main course and lastly the dessert. In Iran, there is no strict order to follow; people serve themselves as they like. As already mentioned, everything except sweets are served and brought to the table at the same time; the table will be full of colourful dishes of *aash*, *khoresh* and rice accompanied by bowls of yogurt, salads, pickles and plates of fresh herbs and feta cheese. Persians love nibbles, both sweet and savoury. Entering any traditional sitting room in Iran, you will find a bowl of fruit, several plates of sweet nibbles, pistachio nuts and bowls of mixed dried fruit arranged on the coffee table. For dinner parties and festivities an array of appetising nibbles is set on the table. These include olives marinated in pomegranate syrup with ground walnuts; a bowl of cucumber yogurt and mint; a large plate of mixed fresh herbs, small red radishes and feta cheese; and a stack of flatbread cut into rectangular pieces. A large bowl of pistachios mixed with other nuts, called *aagil*, is a must.

Shirini means sweet things. The meal ends with black, often aromatic, tea and home-made sweet nibbles including almond marzipan (*toot*, p. 230) *baklava* and *suhan* (p. 237). Jams are also eaten as desserts on their own or with yogurt.

Although Persians do not follow the strict separation of courses that is customary in the West, appetisers are always set out individually on a different table and eaten before the main meal. Some appetisers, like cucumber and yogurt, function as accompaniments and are therefore placed on the main table as well.

Cos lettuce with *sekanjabin*

Cos lettuce heart
with vinegar syrup

Kahoo sekanjebin

Crisp cos lettuce is a favourite in Iran and widely used.
Traditionally it is eaten as an appetiser with vinegar or
vinegar syrup (*sekanjabin* – see the recipe in *New Persian
Cooking*). Nowadays, on account of Western influence,
lettuce is used in salads as well.

In our house we always had cos lettuce with *sekanjabin*
before lunch, while sitting on the balcony in the warm
winter sunshine with my father, reading poetry.

You can find wonderful crisp lettuces of all kinds in
supermarkets. I generally use the variety called Romaine,
which is similar to the Persian cos lettuce.

PREPARATION

Two lettuces will serve four people. Discard the larger outer
leaves, and place the hearts in cold water for 10 minutes; pat
dry and arrange in a flat tray or dish. For the vinegar dip,
pour about ½ cup of balsamic or any other type of vinegar
of your taste in a small bowl. Alternatively use *sekanjabin*.
Separate a leaf or two, dip in the vinegar and eat.

Olives with walnuts in pomegranate syrup

Zeiton parvardeh

PREPARATION about 10 minutes plus chilling in the fridge

INGREDIENTS

200 g/7 oz small green olives (stoned if preferred)
100 ml/3½ fl oz pomegranate syrup
50 g/2 oz crushed walnuts
4 cloves of garlic, crushed
juice of ½ lemon
1 teaspoon dried mint
1 teaspoon *golpar* (*see* INGREDIENTS; can be replaced with thyme)

Olives are grown in the northern provinces on the Caspian Sea. This dish is a speciality of Gilan province. It is made with small green olives and the special herbs of the region.

You can choose any type of green olive, but not the large queen type.

PREPARATION

In a large bowl mix all the ingredients, stir to cover the olives with walnuts and pomegranate syrup and other ingredients. Leave in the fridge for a couple of hours. Serve in a small decorated bowl. You can keep *zeiton parvardeh* in the fridge for a week in a sealed container.

Boiled broad beans in their pods with *golpar*

Baghala ba golpar

Broad beans are very popular in Iran and cooked in many different ways. Broad beans with dill rice is one of the most popular rice dishes (the recipe can be found in *New Persian Cooking*).

This is a wonderful appetiser in summer when the best broad beans are available.

Ground *golpar* is available ready-made in Persian or Middle Eastern food stores.

My family love to gather in the garden on summer evenings and have this dish as an accompaniment to their cocktails.

PREPARATION AND COOKING

Wash the broad bean pods. Take a large saucepan and fill two-thirds with water, bring to the boil. Add the broad beans and the salt, bring back to the boil. Reduce the heat, cover and simmer for 15 20 minutes until the beans are cooked; test by taking one of the beans out and pushing a fork through it – it should be *al dente*.

Drain the beans in a large colander, place under cold running water for a minute until cool to the touch.

Serve in a large tray with small side plates of *golpar* and salt.

To eat, place some on a plate, take the beans out of their pods, dip in salt and *golpar*. (You can remove the skin from the beans themselves if you wish.)

SERVES 4–6
PREPARATION AND
  COOKING about 30 minutes

INGREDIENTS
1 kg/2¼ lb fresh broad beans
  in their shells
2 teaspoons salt
1 teaspoon ground *golpar*
  (*see* INGREDIENTS)

Yogurt, cucumber and mint

Maast va khiar

SERVES 4–6
PREPARATION about
    10 minutes

INGREDIENTS

250 g/9 oz cucumber,
    preferably the small Middle
    Eastern type
½ small red onion
200 g/7 oz Greek-style
    full-fat/whole milk yogurt
1 teaspoon dried mint
1 pinch of chopped fresh herbs
    (parsley, tarragon, basil,
    chives; mix and match as
    available)
1 tablespoon lemon juice
salt and pepper

This is a very popular dish, which is served both as an appetiser and as a side dish.

My recipe is slightly different from the traditional version as it uses other herbs in addition to mint. I prefer to chop rather than grate the cucumber to prevent the dish from becoming too watery.

PREPARATION

Grate or chop the cucumber. Peel and grate the onion.

Mix all the ingredients thoroughly, taste and adjust the seasoning and serve in a clear glass bowl.

Yogurt with wild shallots

Maast va moosir

PREPARATION about
   10 minutes plus soaking
   time

INGREDIENTS

50 g/2 oz dried wild shallots
250 g/9 oz Greek-style yogurt
juice of ½ lime
salt and pepper

Moosir is dried wild shallot. Yogurt with wild shallots is a favourite accompaniment to many meat dishes, especially *chelo kabab*. It originates in the provinces on the Caspian Sea where the wild shallot was prevalent.

Dried wild shallots can be obtained from Persian food stores.

PREPARATION

Soak the shallots in cold water for 2–3 hours to soften them. Finely chop them and place in a bowl. Add the yogurt, lime juice and salt and pepper to taste. Chill for a couple of hours in the fridge before serving.

Fresh herbs, feta cheese and walnuts with flatbread

Naan paneer sabzi

Freshly picked herbs with radishes and spring onions are the staple accompaniments to almost all meals in Iran. Combined with fresh walnuts, feta and flatbread (*lavash*) this is a flavour-rich, delicious appetiser. It is a 'must have' appetiser for dinner parties and festive occasions.

The most common fresh herbs for this dish include mint, tarragon, Persian basil, chives, flat-leaf parsley; these are served with small red radishes and spring onions.

PREPARATION

Wash the herbs thoroughly and dry them in paper kitchen towel (you can store them wrapped in moist towel in the fridge for almost 24 hours).

Cut the feta cheese into small pieces.

On a large tray assemble the ingredients, placing the herbs, radishes and spring onions in one corner neatly, and the walnut halves and the feta cheese on the other side. Place the bread pieces in a bread basket. You can also wrap all the ingredients in flatbread and eat as a sandwich.

SERVES 4–6
PREPARATION about 15–20 minutes

INGREDIENTS

1 bunch each of mint, tarragon, Persian basil, chives, flat leaf parsley, small red radishes and spring onions
200 g/7 oz feta cheese
150 g/5 oz shelled walnut halves
1 large *lavash* bread cut into rectangular pieces (available in Persian or Middle Eastern food stores)

Mixed vegetable pickle

Shoor torshi

This is an easy pickle to make; it involves simply mixing a variety of vegetables with onion, medium-hot green chillies in wine, tarragon or white malt vinegar. You can mix and match any vegetable combinations for this pickle.

PREPARATION

Sterilise the pickling jars: wash, dry and place in the oven at 100°C/210°F for 15 minutes; set to one side to cool.

Peel the onions. Cut the cauliflower into small florets. Peel and cut the carrot into ½ cm/¼ inch discs. Wash and chop the celery. Wash the tarragon.

Dry all the vegetables thoroughly.

Sprinkle the vegetables with salt and the dried herbs, mix all well in a clean bowl and pack them into jars, allowing room for the vinegar; place a couple of sprigs of tarragon in each jar. Now fill the jars with the vinegar of your choice (I prefer tarragon vinegar). Leave a space of about 2 cm/¾ inch at the top. Close tightly and leave for at least three weeks.

MAKES two 500 g/1 lb 2 oz jars.

PREPARATION about 15– 20 minutes plus maturing time

INGREDIENTS

100 g/3½ oz cauliflower florets
100 g/3½ oz celery
4–5 thin green chillies
100 g/3½ oz carrots
8–10 pickling onions
20 g/¾ oz fresh tarragon
½ teaspoon coriander seed
½ teaspoon *golpar* (Persian hogweed)
1 teaspoon dried mint
500 ml/1 pint vinegar
3 teaspoons salt

Garlic pickle

Seer torshi

PREPARATION about 15– 20 minutes plus maturing time

INGREDIENTS

10–12 bulbs of garlic
500 ml/1 pint malt vinegar
1 tablespoon tamarind paste
    with seeds
pickling jars

This is a favourite in our household; my husband loves to make this *torshi* with the help of my sister.

Garlic *torshi* is very popular in northern regions on the Caspian Sea where it is made with vinegar and salt. This recipe is different because we add tamarind paste for additional flavour and also introduce the bacteria necessary for good fermentation. We do not boil the vinegar and do not use salt.

According to the traditional view, garlic *torshi* needs to be matured for seven years to be at its best! Of course you don't need to wait that long – seven months is more than enough. The garlic cloves should be soft at the end of the maturation period.

PREPARATION

Wash your pickling jars, dry them and sterilise in the oven at 100°C/210°F for 15 minutes; set to one side to cool.

Separate the garlic cloves and cut off the top of each clove.

To make the pickling liquid, mix the vinegar thoroughly with the tamarind. Arrange a layer of garlic at the bottom of a sterilised jar, pour some of the liquid over to cover the garlic, add more garlic followed by liquid; continue until the jar is completely full.

Seal and leave in a cool place for at least three months to mature. Garlic pickle keeps well for months, if not years, in a cool place, provided that it is not contaminated during usage.

Tamarind coriander chutney

Chutni-e gashneez

My aunt would make this chutney with hot red chillies, grated onion, fresh coriander leaves in tamarind juice. She usually served it with a fish and herb rice (the recipe for herb rice is in *New Persian Cooking*).

PREPARATION

Peel and grate the onion and chop the chilli. Dissolve 1 tablespoon of tamarind paste in ½ cup of hot water. Wash and dry the coriander, remove the tough stalks, finely chop.

In a small bowl mix all the ingredients, chill in the fridge for half an hour before serving. This pickle is for eating immediately rather than for storing.

SERVES 4
PREPARATION about 10–15 minutes

INGREDIENTS

1 medium onion
20 g/¾ oz fresh coriander leaves
1 hot red or green chilli
1 tablespoon tamarind paste
salt

CHAPTER 7

Side dishes and salads

IN Persia main course meals are always accompanied by a side dish of pickles, yogurt, salad or *sabzi khordan* — a plate of fresh mint, basil, tarragon, spring onions, radishes and parsley. This combination of herbs is often eaten as a sandwich with feta cheese and flatbread (*lavash*) as an appetiser. Yogurt, salad and fresh herbs help to create a healthier and more balanced diet.

Side dishes can be simple or more elaborate and varied according to the occasion.

YOGURT DISHES

Yogurt is an essential part of the Persian diet. No meal is complete without a side dish of either plain yogurt or yogurt combined with fresh or cooked vegetables and/or herbs. Yogurt and jam is a favourite dessert.

Yogurt side dishes are varied, delicious and simple to make. Some – like a mix of cucumber, yogurt and mint – are a ubiquitous part of Persian spreads.

Yogurt combined with cooked and fried vegetables is called *borani*. There are different varieties of *borani* depending on the vegetables used and the addition of herbs and/or garlic.

Most *boranis* can be served as a delicious vegetarian main course or in a smaller portion as a starter.

The base mixture of *borani* is a cooked vegetable mixed with fried onions, garlic and yogurt.

Aubergine with yogurt

Borani-e badenjan

SERVES 4
PREPARATION AND
   COOKING about 30–35
   minutes plus sweating time
   for the aubergine

INGREDIENTS

200 g/7 oz Greek-style yogurt
1 medium aubergine
1 medium onion
3 cloves of garlic
30 ml/2 tablespoons liquid
   saffron (*see* INGREDIENTS)
50 ml/3 tablespoons
   vegetable oil (for frying
   the aubergine; more if
   necessary)
juice of 1 lime

GARNISH

2 dessertspoons dried mint
1 medium onion
4 tablespoons vegetable oil

Aubergine is very much loved in Iran; there are numerous varieties of aubergine dishes, from *khoreshes* to *khoraks*, mixed with egg and served as a side dish with yogurt.

Aubergine *borani* can be a main vegetarian meal or, in a smaller portion, served as a starter.

PREPARATION

Peel and cut the aubergines lengthways into thin slices. Sprinkle with salt and let them sweat for around 15 minutes. Dry them on paper kitchen towel.

Peel and finely chop the onion and the garlic cloves.

COOKING

Fry the aubergine slices, preferably in a non-stick frying pan, to a golden brown (you can use an ordinary frying pan but you will need to use more oil). Remove and dab the aubergine slices dry on paper kitchen towel to absorb any extra oil. Place the aubergines in a bowl and mash them with a wooden spoon.

In the same frying pan fry the chopped onion in a tablespoon of vegetable oil. When golden brown add the chopped garlic, stir and fry for a couple of minutes. Add the roughly mashed aubergine and stir to mix all the ingredients. Turn the heat off, add the yogurt, lemon juice and the saffron, keep warm.

GARNISH

Chop and fry the onion in 2 tablespoons of oil until light brown and put to one side. In another small frying pan, heat up the rest of the oil. Add the dried mint. Stir and remove from the heat immediately.

Serve the *borani* in a shallow bowl and decorate with the garnish.

Broad bean *borani*

Borani-e baghala

Broad beans are used extensively in Persian cooking. Mixed with fresh dill and rice, *baghala polo* (see recipe in *New Persian Cooking*) is a favourite to serve with lamb and is an essential dish for dinner parties and festivities. Broad beans boiled in their pods, eaten with *golpar* (Persian hogweed) and salt, make a delicious snack for summer evenings.

Broad beans combined with yogurt, fried onion, garlic and herbs are a delicious vegetarian starter.

PREPARATION AND COOKING

If using frozen beans, pour boiling water over them, drain and peel off the skin. For fresh beans, remove from the pod and peel off the skin. Fincly chop the onion and the garlic.

Heat the oil in a medium frying pan, fry the onion to golden brown, add the garlic and the broad beans, stir-fry for a couple of minutes. Place the mixture in a bowl, add the yogurt, lemon juice and *golpar*, salt and pepper, mix well and serve.

SERVES 4
PREPARATION
   AND COOKING about
   20–30 minutes

INGREDIENTS

300 g/11 oz shelled fresh or
   frozen broad beans
200 g/7 oz Greek-style yogurt
1 small onion
4 cloves of garlic
1 teaspoon *golpar*
   (*see* INGREDIENTS)
juice of ½ lemon
2 tablespoons olive oil
salt and pepper to taste

Yogurt and purslane *borani*

Borani-e parpin

SERVES 4
PREPARATION AND
COOKING about 20
minutes plus chilling

INGREDIENTS

150 g/5 oz purslane
2 cloves of garlic
1 tablespoon olive oil
200 g/7 oz Greek-style yogurt
1 teaspoon dried mint

Succulent, nutritious leaves of purslane are delicious when added to a green salad or used to make a yogurt side dish.

PREPARATION

Coarsely chop the purslane and the garlic. Heat the oil in a frying pan, fry the garlic first, for a minute, and then the purslane for 2–3 minutes, remove and allow to cool. Transfer to a bowl; add the yogurt and the mint, mix well. Keep in the fridge to chill before serving.

Yogurt, celery and feta cheese mix

Makhloot-e paneer va karafs

The fresh aroma of chopped celery combines well with yogurt mixed with feta cheese. This dish can also be served as a dip.

PREPARATION

Wash and finely chop the celery. In a bowl, crumble the feta cheese, crush the garlic and add to the bowl together with all the other ingredients and mix thoroughly. Taste and adjust the seasoning. Keep in the fridge until ready to serve.

SERVES 4–6
PREPARATION about 10 minutes

INGREDIENTS

150 g/5 oz heart of celery
2 cloves of garlic, crushed
250 g/9 oz Greek-style yogurt
150 g/5 oz feta cheese
1 tablespoon lemon juice
1 teaspoon dried mint
salt and pepper

Auntie Effie's salad

SERVES 4–6
PREPARATION about 30–35
    minutes plus chilling

INGREDIENTS

1 large iceberg lettuce (this
    type of lettuce works best;
    if using cos, select only the
    young crisp leaves, as the
    salad should feel crunchy)
2 large hard-boiled eggs
2 medium oven-roasted
    beetroots (available
    ready-prepared from
    supermarkets)
2 medium onions
4 medium sweet carrots
250 g/9 oz canned red kidney
    beans
450 g/1 lb Greek-style yogurt
3 dessertspoons olive oil
salt and black pepper to taste
1 tablespoon dried mint
    (optional)

This delicious yogurt dish is a combination of very diverse ingredients which together create layers of taste and flavour. It was the speciality of my husband's aunt, who lived in Tehran. I remember her making this dish with great care and attention to detail. I thank Eli, my sister-in-law, for giving me the recipe.

METHOD

Chop the lettuce, eggs, beetroot, carrots and onions into very small pieces (about ½ cm/¼ inch cubes).

Place in a large clear decorative glass salad bowl and add the kidney beans. Sprinkle with salt and pepper and mix well. Add the yogurt and, with a salad spoon, mix all the ingredients with the yogurt. Add the dried mint (optional) and stir to mix with all the ingredients

Note that the yogurt needs to be absorbed into the fabric of the salad. The salad should have a thick creamy consistency.

Leave in fridge. Before serving, give it another toss.

Asparagus, fresh parsley and oregano leaf salad

Salad-e marchubeh

The word 'asparagus' comes from the ancient Persian word *asparag*, meaning sprout, stalk or shoot. Ancient Egyptians cultivated asparagus over 3,000 years ago. It was also cultivated in the eastern Mediterranean region and Asia Minor around 2,000 years ago. Ancient Persians prized asparagus for its medicinal qualities; they ate it fresh when in season.

Nowadays after Western influence it is widely used as an addition to salads.

The combination of asparagus with parsley and oregano goes well with a garlicky citrus dressing and green leaves. This salad can be served as a light starter.

PREPARATION

Bend each asparagus spear so that it snaps at the point where it starts to get woody. Separate the leaves of the parsley and discard the stems. Roughly chop the oregano leaves.

Bring a saucepan of water to the boil, add a tablespoon of salt and place the asparagus in the pan, boil for 3–4 minutes; the tips should be al dente. Remove and cool under running cold water and set to one side.

Assemble the salad in a shallow salad dish by placing the green leaves in first and the asparagus on top.

Make the dressing by placing all the ingredients in a small bowl and beating the mixture with a fork to produce a creamy sauce.

Drizzle the sauce over the salad and serve.

SERVES 4
PREPARATION AND COOKING about 10–15 minutes

INGREDIENTS

500 g/1 lb 2 oz fresh green asparagus
30 g/1 oz flat-leaf parsley
1 tablespoon chopped fresh oregano leaves
1 packet of ready-mixed green leaves (or about 50 g/2 oz any green leaves like watercress or baby spinach)

DRESSING

juice and zest of 1 lemon
2 cloves of garlic, crushed
1 teaspoon Dijon mustard
6 tablespoons extra virgin olive oil
salt and pepper

Mixed pepper, cherry tomato and red onion salad

Salad-e felfel va piaz va gorgehfarangi

SERVES 4–6
PREPARATION about 15–20 minutes

INGREDIENTS

1 yellow pepper (capsicum)
1 large red pepper (capsicum)
1 medium red onion
10–12 cherry tomatoes

DRESSING

juice and zest of 1 large lime
1 pinch of chopped flat parsley
4 tablespoons extra virgin
    olive oil
salt and pepper

This is a refreshing, colourful and appetising salad. The herb citrus dressing adds to the combined flavours of the ingredients. This can be served as a light starter or as a side dish with fish or chicken.

PREPARATION

Wash the peppers and tomatoes and dry them thoroughly with paper kitchen towel.

Peel the onions and slice them as thinly as possible; make sure the slices are round.

With a sharp knife cut the tops off the peppers and remove the seeds, cut each in half and then each half into matchstick-size slices. Halve the cherry tomatoes.

In a shallow salad bowl, carefully mix all the ingredients. Make the dressing in a small bowl and beat with a fork to produce a creamy texture. Drizzle over the salad and toss well.

Carrot, apple, sultana and shredded red cabbage salad

Salad-e seeb, haveej va kalam

SERVES 4–6
PREPARATION about 15–20
minutes

INGREDIENTS

150 g/5 oz red cabbage
150 g/5 oz carrots
2 Granny Smith apples (or any
    tangy green apples)
juice of 1 orange
50 g/2 oz sultanas

DRESSING

juice of 2 small limes
5 tablespoons extra virgin
    olive oil
1 teaspoon sugar
salt and pepper

This a delicious crunchy combination of tangy, juicy apple, sweet sultana and crisp shredded cabbage and carrot, enhanced by lime dressing. Serve in a shallow clear glass dish to show off the vibrant colours. It is ideal as a first course, especially before a fish main course.

PREPARATION

Wash the cabbage, carrots and apples. Soak the sultanas in the orange juice. With a sharp knife shred the cabbage and place in a large salad bowl, then grate the carrots and add to the bowl. Lastly skin and de-core the apples and slice them thinly; add to the mixture of cabbage and carrots. Pour the soaked sultanas with the orange juice into the bowl.

To make the dressing, put all the ingredients in a small bowl and beat to mix thoroughly. Drizzle over the salad and with a salad spoon toss well before serving.

Mashed green lentils with garlic and coriander

Adasi

Lentil dishes are very popular all over Iran. Green lentils are one of the main pulses in some *aashes* (thick soups). Rice with green lentils is a delicious nutritious dish which is made across the country (see the recipe in *New Persian Cooking*).

This dish comes from the famous city of Isfahan in the centre of Iran. It can be served either as a starter or as an appetiser.

PREPARATION AND COOKING

Wash the lentils and drain them. Roughly chop the onion. Finely chop the coriander.

Heat the oil in a medium saucepan; fry the onion lightly for a couple of minutes until translucent. Add the lentils and stir. Add enough boiling water to cover the lentils, bring to the boil, then reduce the heat and simmer for approximately 45 minutes until the lentils are completely cooked and at the point of disintegrating; drive off any extra water and remove from the heat. Leave the lentils to one side to cool a little and then process in a blender or mash. Return to the pan on a low heat, add the butter, the garlic and the coriander, stir and remove from the heat. Add salt and pepper to taste and sprinkle some ground *golpar* over if you wish.

Adasi should be eaten with warm flatbread (*lavash* or pitta).

SERVES 4–6
PREPARATION AND
   COOKING about 1 hour

INGREDIENTS
250 g/9 oz green lentils
1 medium onion
50 g/2 oz chopped coriander/
   cilantro
2 cloves of garlic
1 teaspoon ground *golpar*
   (optional) (*see*
   INGREDIENTS)
1 teaspoon butter
2 tablespoons olive oil
salt and pepper

Potato salad with fresh mint, oregano and capers

Salad-e seebzamini ba aavishan,

na'na va capers

SERVES 4
PREPARATION AND
    COOKING about 25–30
    minutes

INGREDIENTS

1 kg/2¼ lb potatoes
    (preferably salad potatoes)
20 g/¾ oz fresh mint leaves
1 pinch of fresh oregano leaves
    (about 2 teaspoons)
4 spring/salad onions

DRESSING

6 tablespoons extra virgin
    olive oil
juice and zest of 1 large lemon
1 teaspoon Dijon mustard
4 teaspoons capers

This salad is a wonderful dish for a cold buffet. It is also delicious with grilled fish or meat.

PREPARATION AND COOKING

Wash the potatoes and boil them until tender, making sure they do not disintegrate.

Cool them down under running cold water. Peel and cut into 3–4 cm/1½ inch chunks.

Place the chunks in a largish shallow salad bowl. Remove the tough stems of the mint and oregano and chop them roughly; add to the potatoes. Wash and finely chop the spring onions, including the green parts, and add to the bowl.

To prepare the dressing, mix the olive oil, juice and zest of the lemon, mustard and capers. Pour the dressing over the potato and herbs, mix thoroughly with a salad spoon. Garnish with sprigs of oregano and mint.

Chicken salad with sultanas, almonds and tarragon

Salad-e morgh ba tarkhon, keshmesh va baadaam

Chicken with fresh tarragon makes a tasty combination. Sultanas and almonds give this salad additional layers of flavour.

PREPARATION AND COOKING

Wash and dry the chicken breasts. In a small saucepan heat the oil, fry the onion segments for a minute. Add the breasts to the pan, stir, and add enough boiling water to just cover the chicken, simmer for 30 minutes, remove and set to one side to cool.

When cold, shred the chicken in a shallow salad bowl, add all the other ingredients and mix well together.

Make the dressing by beating the mustard with olive oil and the lime juice and zest. Pour the dressing over the chicken and mix thoroughly. Place in the fridge for 30 minutes before serving.

SERVES 4
PREPARATION AND
 COOKING about 45 minutes
 plus chilling

INGREDIENTS

2 skinless chicken breast fillets
1 small onion, peeled and cut
 into 4 segments
1 tablespoon of fresh chopped
 tarragon
30 g/1 oz sultanas
30 g/1 oz almond flakes
2 tablespoons olive oil
salt and pepper

DRESSING

4 tablespoons extra virgin
 olive oil
1 teaspoon mustard
 (English or Dijon)
juice and zest of 1 lime

CHAPTER 8

Sweet things

PERSIANS love sweet nibbles. *Shirini*, or sweet things, are a ubiquitous presence on coffee tables. They are often eaten as snacks or with tea and usually replace desserts.

It is said that the Greeks always referred to Persians as insatiable sweet eaters. Some food historians believe that the habit of ending the meal with sweets originally came from Persia, and was brought to Europe by the crusaders.

Each region in Iran has its own sweet speciality. The most famous is *baghlava* from Yazd, a city in the desert in the centre of the country.

Home-made sweet nibbles, including almond marzipans, *baghlava* and *suhan*, are eaten with black aromatic tea to end the meal. Jams are also eaten as desserts on their own or with yogurt, and sometimes with tea.

Sweet nibbles are a dominant feature of Norooz, the Persian New Year – heralding the arrival of spring on 21 March. Special sweets are prepared; the whole household will be buzzing with activity several weeks beforehand.

For many centuries, Iranians have revered the arrival of spring, at the equinox, taking Norooz as a symbol of rejuvenation and happiness as the earth moves from winter to spring. People would get together, celebrating the arrival of spring, around an arranged table, now known as *Haft-seen*, presenting earth's offerings, from vegetation to minerals to human produce, sharing their joy at a new dawn.

A typical table for a dinner party

Norooz is an occasion wonderfully full with the hustle and bustle of cooking festive food, with the emphasis on sweet things. The traditional meal on New Year's Eve is the sweet and colourful *morassa polo ba morgh,* jewelled rice with saffron chicken, and on New Year's Day *sabzi polo ba maahi,* herb rice with fish. For several weeks beforehand special sweets are prepared and then beautifully presented in decorative dishes for the New Year celebration.

The following sweet nibble recipes are my sister's. Every year she creates the most delicious assortment of sweets for Norooz. Her recipes are a variation on the ones prepared by my aunt in Shiraz – her sweets were famous among relatives and friends for their exquisite taste and presentation.

The ceremonial table of
Persian New Year

Marzipan berries

Toot

PREPARATION about 1 hour

INGREDIENTS
250 g/9 oz ground almonds
250 g/9 oz icing sugar
whisked white of 1 egg
    (organic/free-range)
100 ml/3½ fl oz orange
    blossom water
100 g/3½ oz pistachio slivers
    (for the berry stems)
150 g/5 oz caster sugar (to coat
    the marzipan berries)

In Persian, the mulberry is called *toot*. The marzipan is delicately shaped to resemble white mulberries with a sliver of pistachio inserted at the top to represent the stem of the berry. It is quite time-consuming to carefully shape and finish each individual sweet, but the end result is aesthetically pleasing and delicious.

PREPARATION

Whisk the egg white to a firm consistency; fold in the sugar, beat, and then add the ground almond and the orange blossom water. With your fingers, knead the mixture to make a soft paste.

Take a teaspoon of the paste, place it in the palm of your hand and mould the paste into the shape of a mulberry. Pour a cup of caster sugar onto a large tray or a flat dish and roll the *toot* so they are covered. Insert a pistachio sliver in the top of each mulberry, as the stem. Arrange in circles on a flat decorative dish. You can store the *toot* in an airtight tin for a couple of weeks.

Baklava

Baghlava

PREPARATION AND
COOKING 1½–2 hours

INGREDIENTS

FOR THE PASTRY

(to cover a shallow tin tray
approximately 30 cm by
23 cm/12 by 9 inches)
250 g/9 oz plain flour
2½ tablespoons melted butter
3–4 tablespoons warm water
1 egg yolk
(Alternatively, you can buy
ready-made filo pastry and
follow the instructions on
the packet.)

FOR THE FILLING

200 g/7 oz ground almond
200 g/7 oz caster sugar
1 teaspoon crushed cardamom
seeds
100 g/3½ oz melted unsalted
butter
50 g/2 oz crushed pistachio
nuts

FOR THE SYRUP

180 g/6 oz caster sugar
2 tablespoons rosewater
6 tablespoons water
2 cardamom pods

FOR THE GARNISH

30 g/1 oz crushed pistachio
nuts

Baklava is a well-known sweet in the West. Most Middle
Eastern and Turkish restaurants and confectionary shops sell
it. The Persian version is different. This recipe is a variation
on the traditional one.

The ground almond is delicately flavoured with crushed
cardamom, rosewater and sugar syrup folded into pastry.

PREPARATION AND COOKING

Heat the oven to 180°C/350°F/gas mark 4.

Make the pastry. In a large bowl, beat the egg yolk with
the butter until it turns pale in colour. Add the warm water.
Sift the flour into the bowl and add the egg and water mix.
Knead to make dough (if the dough is too stiff, add more
warm water). Work the dough for approximately 5 minutes,
then cover the bowl with clingfilm and leave for 15 minutes
for the dough to relax. Divide the dough into 4 equal-sized
small balls.

Now prepare the filling by mixing all the ingredients
thoroughly, using your fingers.

Lightly flour a board or work surface and roll one of the
small dough balls into a thin pastry – as thin as possible.
The pastry should be bigger than the tray that you want to
bake the *baghlava* in. Place the pastry on the tray and push
the sides in to completely fill it. Pour ⅓ of the filling mix
onto the pastry and spread it evenly with a large wooden
spoon to cover the whole surface. Prepare the second ball
of dough in the same way as the first and place the pastry
on the filling in the tray. Add a layer of the filling mix and
spread. Repeat the same procedure for the third ball of the

dough, adding the mix between each layer. Finally roll out
the fourth ball of dough and cover the tray with it. Then,
with a sharp knife, cut lengthways, about 2–3 cm/1 inch
apart, across the layers of pastry and then at an angle across
to make diamond-shaped pieces. Baste with melted butter
and bake in the middle of the oven for approximately 30
minutes until the pastry turns golden.

Meanwhile prepare the syrup. Dissolve the sugar with
the water and the cardamom, bring to the boil. Reduce the
heat a little and allow the mixture to simmer gently for 10–15
minutes. Remove from the heat, add the rosewater and set to
one side.

Remove the *baghlava* from the oven and pour the syrup
all over. Let the syrup seep through between the diamond
shapes cut into the baked *baghlava*. Sprinkle the garnish
over. Leave to cool. Carefully remove the diamonds one by
one and arrange in a flat decorated dish. You can store the
baghlava in an airtight container in a cool place for up to
two weeks.

Coconut diamonds

Louze

This delicate sweet has layers of aroma and flavour, combining coconut with almond, laced with rosewater, cardamom and ground pistachio.

PREPARATION

In a large bowl, whisk the egg white until it becomes opaque and stiff. Add the icing sugar, desiccated coconut, ground almonds and rosewater. Mix all the ingredients. You should end up with a thick but soft paste; if you find the paste to be too stiff, add a little more rosewater. Take a medium-sized tray and spread the paste over it to end up with a thickness of approximately 1 cm/½ inch. With a sharp knife cut lengthways into strips about 2 cm/¾ inch apart and then across at an angle at 2 cm/¾ inch intervals, to create diamond-shaped pieces. Sprinkle the ground pistachio and crushed cardamom all over. (Alternatively they can be covered with coconut.) With a spatula carefully separate the diamonds and arrange on a decorative flat plate.

PREPARATION about 20–30 minutes

INGREDIENTS

250 g/9 oz desiccated coconut
100 g/3½ oz ground almonds
350 g/12 oz icing sugar
1 egg, white only (free range/organic)
1 teaspoon crushed cardamom seeds
1 teaspoon ground pistachios
150 ml/5 fl oz rosewater

Honeyed almond sweets

Suhan-e asali

These delicious crunchy sweet bites are uniquely Persian; no other Middle Eastern or Mediterranean cuisine has them. Slivers of almond are cooked in honey and delicately flavoured with saffron and rosewater; then a spoonful of the mix is placed on a buttered cold tray and each piece is garnished with slivers of pistachio. *Suhan* is also made for Norooz. I remember the fun of the many occasions I made *suhan* with my sisters. It is easier when two people make it together: one cooks while the other garnishes the bites as they are spooned on the tray – a job that has to be done quickly.

COOKING

Using 20 g/¾ oz of the butter, lightly grease a large tray and set to one side.

In a heavy-based saucepan melt 80 g of the butter with the sugar and the honey on a medium heat. Add the almond slivers and stir gently and continuously until the almonds start to change colour to light gold and are caramelised. Add the rosewater and saffron, stir rapidly and allow the rosewater to evaporate (it will spit) for approximately 5 minutes. Remove from the heat. Take ½ tablespoon of the mixture and place it on the tray. Test after a minute to see if it has set; if not, cook for a further few minutes and test again. When ready, pour a tablespoon at a time onto the tray and garnish quickly with the pistachio slivers. When cold, arrange in a shallow bowl. *Suhan* can be stored in an airtight tin for up to a month.

This is an easy sweet to make but you must take care that the almonds do not overcaramelise. On the other hand, if you undercook the mixture the sweets will be soft instead of crunchy.

PREPARATION AND
COOKING about 20–30
minutes

INGREDIENTS
200 g/7 oz flaked almonds
100 g/3½ oz clear honey
100 g/3½ oz sugar
100 g/3½ oz unsalted butter
4 teaspoons liquid saffron
(*see* INGREDIENTS)
3 tablespoons rosewater
50 g/2 oz pistachio slivers for
garnish
butter for greasing the tray

ICE CREAMS

I N IRAN, ice cream was traditionally eaten as a refreshing snack on a summer evening. Nowadays ice cream and sorbet are served as a dessert.

The following delicious recipes are provided by John Bateson, my brother-in-law, who has perfected the art of ice cream-making. His rosewater and *sa'alab* ice cream is renowned among our Persian friends, who still remember with nostalgia the Akbar Mashti ice cream of old Tehran.

Saffron ice cream with frozen cream

Bastani zaafrani ba khameh

This may sound like an unusual dish since in the West we tend to associate saffron with savoury rather than sweet dishes. However, a small amount of saffron in an ice cream adds a delicate colour and a distinctive pleasant taste. Mixing ice cream with frozen cream is common in Iran; here it adds a pleasant texture and produces an attractive colour combination.

COOKING

Whip 50 ml/2 fl oz of double cream until it's just stiff. Pour into a plastic container large enough that the cream will be about 1 cm/½ inch deep. Put a lid on the container and freeze until needed. With a standard freezer at −18°C/0°F this will take up to 2 hours. Once frozen it will keep for up to a week.

Put the milk, the remaining 300 ml/10 fl oz of cream, sugar and saffron in a large saucepan. Bring to the boil, stirring to ensure that the sugar dissolves. Reduce the heat to a simmer and reduce the liquid by a quarter, stirring frequently. This will probably take 20–25 minutes. Add the evaporated milk and cool the mixture as quickly as possible by standing the bowl in a sink of cold water and stirring the mixture. Sieve and place in a sealed container in a fridge to chill thoroughly. The mixture can be kept overnight if necessary.

Churn in an ice-cream maker following the manufacturer's instructions. See below for instructions on making this recipe without an ice-cream maker.

MAKES about 800 ml/1½ pints of mixture (enough for a 1.1 litre/1¾ pint ice-cream machine)

PREPARATION 20–30 minutes, plus time needed for chilling and churning

INGREDIENTS

350 ml/12 fl oz double cream
400 ml/14 fl oz whole or full fat milk
1 tablespoon of saffron liquid
100 g/3½ oz granulated sugar
250 ml/9 fl oz unsweetened evaporated milk

Wait until the ice cream is sufficiently stiff that it stops the blades or the machine indicates that the ice cream is ready. Scoop the ice cream into a chilled bowl. Remove the frozen cream from the freezer and place the container in a sink of warm water long enough to free the cream. Place on a chopping board and, using a sharp knife, cut into 1 cm/½ inch cubes (don't worry if the cream splinters as long as there are some cubes). Tip the cream into the ice cream and fold in using a spoon or spatula. The aim is to have small lumps of cream spread throughout the ice cream. You need less than in a typical chocolate chip ice cream. If you add them too early they will melt. (It still makes the ice cream taste good!) Put the ice cream in a container and return to the freezer for an hour to achieve the right consistency.

THE TRAY METHOD

It is possible to make ice cream without a machine using the tray method. Pour the ice cream mixture into a chilled freezer container, preferably so that the ice cream is between 2.5 and 4 cm/1 and 2 inches deep. Put the lid on the container and put in the freezer for 2 hours until the mixture is frozen around the edges and on the bottom but soft in the middle (2 hours should be about the correct time in a domestic freezer set at −18°C/0°F). Scrape the soft mixture into a chilled mixing bowl and beat using an electric mixer. Return quickly to the container and put back into the fridge for 1½–2 hours. Repeat the beating and then return to the freezer for a minimum of 1 hour.

To add frozen cream to this version of the recipe, wait for 1 hour after the last beating and then turn the ice cream into a chilled bowl. Prepare and add the chips of frozen cream as described above.

Cardamom ice cream

Bastani-e hel

This ice cream has a very Middle Eastern flavour. Providing the proportions are correct this recipe makes for a very delicate and intriguing flavour.

This ice cream can be made using a number of different recipes. I find the best flavour comes from using a custard mixture and infusing the cardamom in the milk.

PREPARATION

Put the cardamom pods into a mortar and gently crush the green outer pods with the pestle. Remove as much of the pod as possible, leaving only the black seeds. Grind the seeds to a fine powder.

COOKING

Place the milk and ground cardamom seeds in a small pan. Heat until the milk is just boiling, then turn off the heat, cover the pan and allow the mixture to infuse for a maximum of 1 hour. (Leaving the mixture longer increases the cardamom flavour.)

In a medium bowl whisk together the egg yolks and the sugar until they form a creamy yellow mixture. Strain the milk through a fine sieve (don't worry if the ground cardamom seeds pass through the sieve). Reheat the milk and when just boiling whisk into the egg mixture. Place the bowl over a pan of simmering water (make sure than the bottom of the bowl does not touch the water) or use a bain-marie. Stir the mixture with a non-metallic spoon until it thickens (this should take approximately 30 minutes). The easiest way to determine when it has thickened is to stir the

MAKES about 700 ml/1¼ pints of the mixture (enough for a 1.1 litre/1¾ pint ice-cream machine)

PREPARATION 20 minutes, plus time needed for chilling and churning

INGREDIENTS

375 ml/14 fl oz whole/full-fat milk
250 ml/9 fl oz whipping cream
3 egg yolks
100 g/3½ oz sugar
2 tablespoons cardamom seeds

mixture, turn the spoon over and run your finger across the back of the spoon. The mixture is thickened if the finger leaves a line that stays and the mixture does not flow. If you have a good digital thermometer, you can cook the mixture directly over the heat. Raise the temperature to 85°C/185°F and hold it there for a couple of minutes. (Take care: at about 88°C/190°F the egg starts to scramble! If you think the mixture is overheating, plunge the bowl into a sink of cold water and stir vigorously to ensure a smooth custard.) Remove the custard from the heat and cool as quickly as possible by standing in a sink of cold water and stirring.

Sieve the finished custard again and add the whipping cream. Chill in the fridge. You can keep it overnight if necessary. Make into ice cream using a machine or use the tray method (p. 240).

Serve sprinkled with dried rose petals if you have them.

Melon ice cream

Bastani-e talebi

This is a very easy ice cream to make, provided that you can source a ripe melon. Stick to the strongly flavoured varieties such as cantaloupe or charente and make sure you choose one that is ripe. An overripe melon can also be used, provided that it has not begun to rot.

PREPARATION

Cut the melon in half and scoop out the seeds with a slotted spoon, keeping as much of the juice as possible. Over the bowl of a food processor or blender, scoop out the ripe melon flesh and juice. Add the lemon juice and blend to a smooth purée. Measure out 250 ml/9 fl oz of the purée. (The rest serves well as the base for a smoothie.) Place in a covered container in the refrigerator to cool.

COOKING

Following the recipe for cardamom ice cream above (p. 241), make custard using the whole milk, sugar and egg yolks. Sieve the custard and place in the fridge to cool.

To assemble the ice cream mix the melon purée, custard and whipping cream and stir well. Add the mixture to an ice-cream machine and follow the manufacturer's instructions (or use the tray method, p. 240). Return the mixture to the container, seal and freeze for 30 minutes to obtain the correct consistency

MAKES about 750 ml/1¼ pints of mixture (enough for a 1.1 litre/1¾ pint ice-cream machine)

PREPARATION 20–30 minutes, plus time needed for chilling and churning

INGREDIENTS

1 whole melon
juice of 1 lemon
250 ml/9 fl oz whole milk
150 g/5 oz granulated sugar
2 egg yolks
250 ml/9 fl oz whipping cream

VARIATIONS

This recipe can be used to make a delicious peach ice cream provided that you can find really ripe peaches. Sometimes it is easier to find ripe nectarines, which can be substituted.

Plunge the peaches or nectarines into a pan of boiling water for a maximum of 1 minute. Remove with a slotted spoon and place in a bowl of cold water. The skins should then come off very easily. Remove the stones and mix with the lemon juice in a food processor. Then follow the melon recipe.

Date and orange ice cream

Bastani-e porteghal va khorma

Oranges and dates are to be found in every Persian household. They are not often combined into an ice cream but it creates a beautiful flavour combination reminiscent of summer days. This recipe again uses the custard method to make the ice-cream base, since the milk can be used to make an orange zest infusion.

PREPARATION

Wash the skins of the oranges with warm water. Rinse and dry them. Skin and de-stone the dates. Slice them in four lengthways and then chop into small pieces, the size of chocolate chips in chocolate-chip ice cream.

COOKING

Place the milk in a pan and, using a grater or zester, add the zest from all three oranges. Split the vanilla pod in half along its length and scrape the seeds into the milk. Add the vanilla pods. Slowly bring the milk to the boil and then turn off the heat, cover the pan and leave for 30–40 minutes to infuse.

In the meantime juice the three oranges and place the juice in another pan. Bring to the boil and simmer until the volume has reduced by half. Place in a container in the fridge to cool thoroughly.

In a medium-sized bowl beat the egg yolks and sugar together. Strain the orange and vanilla through a fine sieve; don't worry if the vanilla seeds and orange zest escape. Bring the milk back to the boil and whisk it into the sugar and egg mixture. Place over simmering water and cook the custard (see the recipe for cardamom ice cream on p. 241). Place the

MAKES 850 ml/1½ pints of mixture (enough for a 1.1 litre/1¾ pints ice-cream machine)

PREPARATION 1½ hours, plus time needed for chilling and churning

INGREDIENTS

500 ml/1 pint whole milk
3 large oranges (unwaxed; blood oranges make the dish even more exciting to look at)
3 egg yolks
1 vanilla pod (or a teaspoon of vanilla essence)
12 fresh dates (such as medjool or any fresh date from a Middle Eastern shop)
250 ml/9 fl oz whipping cream
200 g/7 oz sugar

custard in the fridge to cool. (If using vanilla essence add it now, once the mixture has cooled.)

Assemble the ice-cream mixture by combining the custard, reduced orange juice and whipping cream. Place in an ice-cream maker and run until the ice cream is thick enough that the blades are unable to churn any more. Remove the ice cream to a bowl and stir in the chopped dates, ensuring that they are evenly spread. (If stir-freezing the mixture without a machine, add the dates when you are whipping the ice cream for the last time.)

Rosewater *sa'alab* ice cream

Bastani-e golaab ba sa'alab

This ice cream is popular throughout Iran and in the Iranian diaspora around the world. It has a unique consistency and is almost elastic when scooped or eaten. This consistency comes from the *sa'alab* itself.

Sa'alab is made from the ground bulbs of a wild orchid. The orchid has two adjoining bulbs: the larger one feeds the orchid, the second is a spare. Traditionally shepherds, whilst minding their goats or sheep, would carefully raise the orchid and remove the spare bulb. Once replanted the orchid regenerates its spare bulb.

The bulbs are boiled in water or milk and air-dried. Finally the dried orchid is ground to make *sa'alab*. It takes some 1,000 orchids to make 1 kg/2¼ lb of *sa'alab*. This ice cream was invented in Tehran some sixty years ago. It has now become so popular that the future of the orchid is threatened. Indeed Turkey, home of many lovers of this ice cream, has banned the export of *sa'alab* in order to preserve its dwindling orchid population! Nevertheless it can still be bought from Middle Eastern shops. Although it is expensive, only a small amount is needed.

MAKES enough for a 1.1 litre/1¾ pint ice-cream machine

PREPARATION 10–15 minutes, plus time needed for chilling and churning

INGREDIENTS

500 ml/1 pint whole milk
250 g/9 oz granulated sugar
2 teaspoons *sa'alab*
1–2 tablespoons of rosewater to taste

PREPARATION

Put the milk in the fridge and chill. Put the milk, sugar and *sa'alab* into a food processor or blender. Blend enough to dissolve the sugar and *sa'alab*. This will take more time than you might expect as the *sa'alab* is not very soluble and will sink to the bottom if the mixture is left for any time. Aim for a smooth liquid with no lumps. At the very end, stir in the rosewater. Add to the ice-cream maker as soon as possible. This is one of the few ice creams that cannot be made successfully without a machine since the churning of the machine keeps the *sa'alab* evenly spread.

If you prefer to keep the mixture for later, chill in the fridge, but blend again immediately before adding to the ice-cream maker.

Scoop the ice cream into a container and freeze for at least 1 hour to achieve the right consistency. When storing the ice cream make sure to remove it from the freezer half an hour before serving.

I tried for a long time to re-create this ice cream. There are many recipes, most of which involve cooking the *sa'alab* into some form of custard. None produced the famous ice cream I remembered. I am indebted to Margaret Shaida, whose recipe from *The Legendary Cuisine of Persia* showed me that the *sa'alab* does not need to be cooked. I was finally able to create an ice cream to rival those in my memory.

VARIATIONS

The ice cream can be made plain without the rosewater. It can then be served sprinkled with chopped pistachios or grated bitter chocolate

Alternatively add 1 tablespoon of liquid saffron to the mixture instead of the rosewater. This adds a delicious favour and colour.

With or without the saffron the ice cream can be made even more delicious by adding frozen cream (see the recipe for saffron ice cream with frozen cream, p. 239).

Date halva

Halva khormaee

This is a rich dessert from the southern regions of the country. It is very popular in Bushehr, where they have wonderful dates.

You can find good quality dates in Persian or Middle Eastern shops; alternatively use medjool dates.

PREPARATION AND COOKING

Remove the stones and flatten the dates with the back of a large spoon.

In a frying pan mix the flour with the oil and place the pan on a medium heat. Stir the mixture continuously until golden brown. Now add the dates, the cinnamon and the walnuts. Stir well to mix all the ingredients. Cook for a further 3–4 minutes to obtain a smooth consistency, remove from the heat and serve in a flat dish. With a spatula flatten the mixture to the thickness of 1–2 cm/¾ inch to cover the surface of the plate. Sprinkle the two garnishes all over. With a sharp knife, cut into diamond-shaped pieces while still warm, and arrange in a decorative dish.

SERVES 4–6
PREPARATION
    AND COOKING about
    15–20 minutes

INGREDIENTS

500 g/1 lb 2 oz dates
250 g/9 oz plain flour
150 ml/5 fl oz vegetable oil
100 g/3½ oz crushed walnuts
1 teaspoon cinnamon

GARNISH

20 g/¾ oz desiccated coconut
20 g/¾ oz pistachio slivers

Rice cream

Fereni

SERVES 4
PREPARATION AND
  COOKING about 25–30
  minutes

INGREDIENTS
500 ml/1 pint milk
100 g/3½ oz rice flour
  (available in supermarkets;
  be sure to buy flour
  made only from white
  rice – a similar flour made
  for people with gluten
  intolerance contains both
  brown and white rice and is
  intended for baking)
70 g/2½ oz sugar
3 tablespoons rosewater

GARNISH
1 tablespoon crushed pistachio

The best translation of *fereni* is that suggested by Margaret Shaida in her book *The Legendary Cuisine of Persia*: 'rice cream'.

This is a fragrant, smooth, light and comforting dessert. For me, it brings back many special childhood memories.

Although easy to make, *fereni* needs continuous attention and should be cooked gently over a low heat with patience. The mixture of rice flour and milk tends to go lumpy if not stirred constantly.

PREPARATION AND COOKING

Mix the rice flour with some of the cold milk (3–4 tablespoons) to make a smooth paste.

Place the rest of the milk in a saucepan on a low heat and bring to the boil, add the rice paste while stirring continuously. Make sure that the heat is low to prevent the mixture becoming lumpy. Keep stirring for 10–15 minutes until the mixture begins to thicken, then add the sugar and the rosewater. Continue to stir and cook for a further 5 minutes. The texture should be like double cream, smooth and shiny. Remove from the heat and serve in a clear glass bowl, garnish with crushed pistachio.

Fereni is at its best when chilled.

Orange blossom rice pudding

Sheer berenj

The traditional version of this pudding is made with cardamom and rosewater, but I prefer my mother's version. She added orange flower water instead of rosewater and omitted the cardamom. The orange blossom scent gives the dish a delicate flavour.

PREPARATION AND COOKING

Wash the rice several times and soak in water for a couple of hours. Pour the water into a saucepan, add the rice with a teaspoon of salt and bring to the boil. Reduce the heat and allow to simmer until the rice is almost soft. Add the milk and bring back to the boil, then reduce the heat and cook for a further 20 minutes on a low heat, stirring gently from time to time until the consistency of the mixture becomes creamy. Remove from the heat and add the orange blossom water, stir well and serve in a bowl. Garnish with almond and pistachio slivers. Allow to chill completely in the fridge before eating.

Rice pudding is usually eaten with morello cherry jam.

SERVES 4–6

PREPARATION AND COOKING about 20–30 minutes plus soaking and chilling

INGREDIENTS

200 g/7 oz rice (any type)
750 ml/1¼ pints full fat milk
200 ml/7 fl oz water
400 g/14 oz sugar
2 tablespoonfuls orange flower water

GARNISH

20 g/¾ oz mix of pistachio slivers and flaked almonds

JAMS

IN IRAN, jam (*morabba*) is a delicacy, translucent, fragrant and colourful. Jams are made from a range of fruits such as morello cherries, figs, quince, apple and vegetables like carrot and cucumber, along with rose petals and orange blossom.

Jams are eaten with ice cream, with yogurt, and are served with tea at the end of the meal.

Home-made jams should be stored in sterilised jars, preferably in a cool and dark place. They keep well, provided that they are not contaminated during usage.

Morello cherry jam
Morabba-e aalbaloo

These cherries are very different to dessert cherries; they are tart if eaten raw. They do, however, make a delicious jam. The added advantage is that you can reserve some of the syrup to use as a cordial or, as my family is prone to do, drink mixed with vodka.

Morello cherries are also used to make the delicious morello cherry rice, *aalbaloo polo* (see the recipe in *New Persian Cooking*).

PREPARATION

Unless you have infinite patience you will need a cherry stoner. This little hand-held gadget is available online and will save you hours of work. Wash the cherries and remove the stalks. De-stone the cherries and then weigh them. You need the same weight in sugar. Put the stones to one side.

Put the cherries in a pan or bowl that will fit in your refrigerator. Pour 250 g/9 oz of the sugar over the cherries and put in the fridge for at least 12 hours to draw the juices out. Wrap the stones in a piece of muslin or cloth and tie securely with string (you don't want them escaping into the jam after all that effort to take them out).

Put the cherries and the juice into a pan large enough to hold them and not be more than half-full. Top up the sugar so that you have the same weight of sugar as cherries. Add 150 ml/5 fl oz of water and the bag of cherry stones (they enhance the flavour of the jam).

Bring to the boil and then turn down to a simmer for 15 minutes. Stir all the time to make sure that the cherries do not stick. At this point test a cherry: it should still be

MAKES approximately
1 kg/2¼ lb of jam, or 3
medium-sized jars

INGREDIENTS
500 g/1 lb 2 oz stoned cherries
(you will need
approximately 750 g/
1 lb 10 oz of cherries
with stones in)
juice of 2 lemons
500 g/1 lb 2 oz granulated
sugar

firm but be cooked. If not, simmer for a little longer. Avoid overcooking or the cherries will disintegrate. Remove the cherry stones and discard.

Bring the mixture back to the boil. If you are going to remove some syrup, now is the time to take it out carefully with a ladle. Adjust the heat to create a steady rolling boil for about 10 minutes. Carefully stir from time to time to prevent sticking, looking out for splashes.

Use a sugar thermometer to test for a set. Alternatively pour a little of the mixture onto a plate that you have had in the freezer; a set has been reached when the jam forms a skin that wrinkles when you push it with a finger.

Allow the jam to stand for 15 minutes so that the cherries absorb the syrup and there is less chance of them floating to the top of the jam. Ladle the jam into sterilised jars.

VARIATIONS

This jam is delicious with vanilla. Cut a pod open lengthways and scrape out the seeds. Add the pod and the seeds to the cherries when you first cook them. Take the pod out before putting the jam in jars. Alternatively remove the ends of the pod and discard; cut the rest into 1 cm/½ inch lengths and add to the cherries. The cooked pods can stay in the jam.

Some people advocate the addition of 25 ml/2 tablespoons of brandy just before putting the jam into the jars. The effect is to mellow the taste and give it depth.

Morello cherries usually have enough natural pectin to ensure a set (unlike dessert cherries), particularly if the stones are used as described. Indeed I have never added pectin. If you want to make doubly sure you can use jam sugar with added pectin, or add a packet of pectin and follow the supplier's instructions.

Fig jam

Morabba-e angeer

The fig is a much-loved fruit in Iran. Fresh figs are small, wonderfully juicy and sweet.

Dried fig mixed with dried white mulberries, pistachios and almonds is called 'sweet *aajil*'. It is often present on coffee tables and is eaten as a snack. Dried fig is also used for stuffing and for making jewelled rice.

PREPARATION

This recipe works with any kind of fig. Really ripe figs tend to disintegrate; less ripe ones maintain some shape. Top and tail the figs, quarter and then cut each quarter in half. (I include the skins but if you have the patience you can peel them.)

Place the figs and the sugar in a bowl and add the vanilla pod. Mix and leave overnight in the fridge to allow the juices to flow.

COOKING

Place the fig mixture in a pan. Zest and juice the lemon and add to the pan. Bring to the boil. Turn down to an active simmer and cook until the mixture reaches 104°C/220°F or the setting point (see the morello cherry jam, previous recipe), approximately 40 minutes.

Carefully remove the vanilla pod and run under cold water to cool. Split the pod in half and scrape the seeds into the jam. (You can also top and tail the pod, cut it into 1 cm/½ inch lengths and add to the jam).

Pour the jam into sterilised jars. Seal when cooled.

MAKES two 350 g/12 oz jars

INGREDIENTS

500 g/1 lb 2 oz black or
    green figs
350 g/12 oz caster sugar
1 lemon
1 vanilla pod

Cucumber jam

Morabba-e khiar

MAKES one 350g jar

INGREDIENTS

250g/9oz cucumbers
    (preferably the small
    Middle Eastern variety)
300g/11oz sugar
100ml/3½floz water
2 teaspoons rosewater

Cucumbers in Iran are small, tender and delicately aromatic. This jam is both aesthetically pleasing and flavoursome. My aunt in Shiraz made this jam beautifully. I still remember the elaborate tray that contained an array of colourful jams in small decorated clear glass bowls, brought in at the end of the meal with the tea in small slender glasses (*estekans*).

PREPARATION

Peel the cucumbers and cut them in half lengthways. Scoop out the seeds with a spoon and then slice each half lengthways into three or four pieces. Cut the strips of cucumber into 5–6cm/2–3 inch lengths. For larger cucumbers adopt the same approach but ensure that they end up in pieces less than 1cm/½ inch across by 5–6cm/2–3 inches long.

COOKING

Place the sugar and half the water into a small pan. Heat and stir to dissolve the sugar. Place the cucumber and the rest of the water into a different pan and parboil for 5 minutes. Add the cucumber and rosewater to the syrup and bring to the boil. Allow to cool, then pour into a sterilised jar. Keep somewhere cool.

Carrot jam

Morabba-e haveej

MAKES one 350 g jar

INGREDIENTS

180 g/6 oz carrots
200 ml/7 fl oz water
150 g/5 oz sugar
3 cardamom pods
2 teaspoons rosewater
¼ teaspoon vanilla essence

This was the favourite jam in our house. My mother made this jam perfectly; it was wonderfully delicate and fragrant.

PREPARATION

Peel the carrots and cut into juliennes about 5 cm/2 inches long, using a mandolin or sharp knife. You should end up with 150 g/5 oz of juliennes.

Crush the pods of the cardamom and extract the black seeds.

COOKING

Put the carrots into a small pan and add 100 ml/3½ fl oz of water and the cardamom seeds. Bring to the boil and then turn down to a simmer. Stir occasionally until the carrots wilt (3–5 minutes). Meanwhile dissolve the sugar in the remaining water (in a warmed pan if necessary). Add the carrot to the sugar syrup. Bring to the boil. (See the morello cherry jam recipe, p. 257.) Add the rosewater and the vanilla essence and boil briefly. Take off the heat immediately and allow to cool in the fridge for 24 hours before pouring into a sterilised jar.

Ingredients

Advieh

Advieh is a blend of spices that is used to season *khoreshes*, *khoraks* and rice dishes. The blend varies from region to region but usually includes cinnamon, cumin, nutmeg and sometimes ground coriander seeds. *Advieh* is sold in sachets in Middle Eastern and Persian shops.

GENERAL RECIPE

This combination is used in rice recipes as well as in meat recipes from the north:

- 1 teaspoon ground cinnamon
- 1 teaspoon ground cumin
- 1 teaspoon ground cardamom
- 1 teaspoon ground nutmeg
- 1 teaspoon ground rose petals

In the south, instead of rose petals and nutmeg, add:

- 1 teaspoon ground coriander/cilantro
- 1 teaspoon ground fenugreek
- 1 teaspoon ginger (fresh or ground)
- 1 teaspoon turmeric.

Barberry – *Zereshk*

Barberries are the bright red fruit of a thorny shrub *Berberis vulgaris*. They are used dried. The ruby-red, almost translucent, sour berries are used in a number of traditional dishes, the most common being *zereshk polo* (see *New Persian Cooking*) and *morassa polo* (p. 143). *Zereshk* is sold in sachets in Persian and Middle Eastern shops.

PREVIOUS SPREAD
Barberries
LEFT *Advieh*

Fenugreek – *Shanbaleeleh*

Fenugreek leaves are used as a herb, both fresh and dried, and the seeds are ground as a spice. In Persian cooking the leaves are used more often than the seeds. I prefer dried fenugreek because of its stronger, more intense aroma in dishes such as the traditional soup *eshkeneh* (p. 44). Sachets of dried fenugreek are sold in Persian shops.

Golpar

Meaning literally the 'wing of a flower', *golpar* (*Heracleum persicum*, Persian hogweed) grows wild in the mountainous regions of Iran. The ground seed pods are used as a spice, aromatic and tasty, sprinkled on snacks and vegetable dishes such as cooked broad beans/fava beans, and on fresh fruit, such as pomegranate seeds. *Golpar* is sold in sachets in Middle Eastern and Persian shops; it is sometimes (wrongly) referred to as angelica seeds.

Kashk

Kashk is sun-dried whey, left over after butter-making; it is mixed with water before serving. It has the highest concentration of protein of any dairy product. In Iran, butter is extracted from diluted yogurt, *doogh*. A generous measure of salt is added to the remaining liquid. It is poured into a muslin bag, drained to a paste, rolled into ping-pong-sized balls and left to dry rock hard in the sun.

Nowadays Middle Eastern or Persian shops sell powdered or liquid *kashk* in bottles,which you can mix with water before use.

Kashk is an acquired taste. My Western guests have almost always remarked on the unusual flavour of dishes that have *kashk* in them.

Limoo amaani

Dried limes – *Limoo amaani*

Dried limes, *limoo amaani*, are exclusively a Persian ingredient; no other cuisine uses them. They give a distinctive aroma and flavour to meat dishes; they are essential ingredients in some *khoreshes* and *khoraks*. Dried limes may be used either whole or in powdered form. You can buy dried limes from Persian food shops.

Pomegranate syrup – *Robb-e anaar*

Pomegranate syrup, also known as pomegranate molasses, pomegranate paste or *robb-e anaar*, is a main ingredient of many sweet-and-sour dishes.

Bottles of concentrated pomegranate syrup are sold in Middle Eastern and Persian shops and some supermarkets.

Saffron – *Za'fran*

Saffron, intensely aromatic and colourful, is one of the distinctive constituents of Persian cuisine. It is used perhaps more than any other spice. Saffron is often added to a dish while it is cooking to enhance the flavour and add depth and complexity to the aroma. A spoonful of this golden liquid, drizzled over the food just before serving, provides a dash of vibrant colour and adds the finishing touch to many dishes.

LIQUID SAFFRON

Before use, grind the saffron strands with granulated sugar using a pestle and mortar. Saffron is usually sold in 1 gram boxes or jars. You can grind the whole content of the package with 1 teaspoon of granulated sugar to a fine powder and keep it in an airtight jar. If you are not sure of the quantity, grind ½ teaspoon of saffron strands with ¼ teaspoon of granulated sugar. I brew the saffron powder like tea in order to extract as much of the aroma and flavour as possible. In a cup, mix ¼ teaspoon of the powder with four tablespoons of boiling water. Stir with a teaspoon, cover the

Liquid saffron

cup and allow to brew for 3 or 4 minutes before use. You can keep the liquid in the fridge for up to a week. Keep the box or the sachet in the freezer.

Sumac

Sumac is a spice made from the red berries that appear in dense clusters on a bush that grows wild throughout Iran. The berries are dried and crushed to form a coarse purple-red powder. *Sumac* has a distinct and slightly aromatic sour taste. In Iran, *sumac* is used as a condiment, sprinkled on *chelo kabab*.

Sumac powder is sold in Middle Eastern shops; it is also available in larger supermarkets.

Tamarind – *Tamr-e hendi*

In Persian cooking, tamarind is used in dishes from the south which reflect the influence of Indian cuisine.
You can buy tamarind in various forms, but the best type to use for Persian cooking is packaged concentrated tamarind with seeds. Two kinds are quite widely available in specialist shops and larger supermarkets: the Indian version, which is more tangy; and the Thai version, which is sweeter.

PREPARATION

Put 2 teaspoons of tamarind paste into a small bowl and add about 150 ml/5 fl oz of hot water. Leave to stand for 10–15 minutes. Stir well to dissolve the paste in the water. Pass the liquid through a fine sieve to separate any stringy bits or stones that might have been left in the paste.

Turmeric – *Zardchobeh*

Turmeric is derived from the rhizomes (root-like stems) of *Curcuma longa*, which are dried and ground for use as a spice. Recently it has been shown that turmeric has potent anti-inflammatory properties. In Persian cooking, turmeric

Turmeric

is used extensively in almost all *aashes*, *khoreshes*, *khoraks* and most rice dishes. It lends its deep yellow colour to the food and accentuates flavours. It also helps reduce the powerful aroma of lamb. Ground turmeric is readily available from supermarkets and Middle Eastern or Indian shops.

Bibliography

Abbott, Jacob, *History of Alexander the Great*, Nathaniel Cooke, London, 1853.

Carter, Charles, *The Compleat City and Country Cook: or Accomplish'd Housewife*, London, 1732 (www.archive.org/stream/compleatcity andoocartgoog).

Daryabandari, Najaf, *Ketab-e Mostatab-e Ashpaᴢi Aᴢ Seer Ta Piaᴢ*, Karnameh Press, Tehran, 2000.

Emami, Goli, *Ashpaᴢi Bedoon-e Goosht*, Niloofar Press, Tehran, 1990.

Hazlitt, W. Carew, *Old Cookery Books and Ancient Cuisine*, Elliot Stock, London, 1886.

Herodotus, *Persian Wars*, Book 7: *Polymnia*, trans. George Rawlinson 1942, ed. Bruce J. Butterfield (www.parstimes.com/history/herodotus/persian_wars/polymnia.html).

Joret, Charles, *Les Plantes dans l'Antiquité et au Moyen Age*, Vol. II: *L'Iran et l'Inde*, Émile Bouillon, Paris, 1904 (www.archive.org/details/lesplantesdansloıjoregoog).

Joret, Charles, *La Rose dans l'Antiquité et au Moyen Age*, Émile Bouillon, Paris, 1892 (www.archive.org/details/larosedanslanti oojoregoog).

Kole, C. (ed.), *Genome Mapping and Molecular Breeding in Plants*, Vol. 4: *Fruits and Nuts*, Springer Verlag, Berlin and Heidelberg, 2007.

Laufer, Berthold, *Sino-Iranica; Chinese Contributions to the History of Civiliᴢation in Ancient Iran*, Field Museum of Natural History, Chicago, 1919 (www.archive.org/stream/sinoiranicachine oolaufrich).

McCormick Spices of the World Cookbook, prepared and tested by Mary Collins, Penguin, London, 1974.

Montazami, Roza, *Honar-e Ashpaᴢi*, Iran Chaap, Tehran, 1969.

Moore, Thomas, *Lallah Rookh*, Longman, Rees, Orme, Brown & Green, London, 1826.

Murray, Hugh, F.R.S.E., *Travels of Marco Polo*, Oliver & Boyd, Edinburgh, 1844.

Neshatoddowleh, Banoo, *Tabbakhi Neshat*, Mesbahi, Tehran, 1972.

Roden, Claudia, *A New Book of Middle Eastern Food*, Penguin, London, 1986.

Shaida, Margaret, *The Legendary Cuisine of Persia*, Grub Street, London, 2004.

This, Hervé, and Pierre Gagnaire, *Cooking, the Quintessential Art*, University of California Press, Berkeley, 2008.

List of recipes

Index